EVERYTHING IS GOING TO BE K.O.

KAIYA STONE

HEAD
ZEUS

First published in the UK in 2020 by Head of Zeus

Text copyright © Kaiya Stone, 2020

9 7 5 3 1 2 4 6 8

A catalogue record for this book is available from
the British Library.

ISBN (HB): 9781789544961
ISBN (E): 9781789544992

Designed and typeset by Ben Prior

Printed and bound in Great Britain by
CPI Group (UK) Ltd, Croydon CR0 4YY

Head of Zeus Ltd
5–8 Hardwick Street
London EC1R 4RG

WWW.HEADOFZEUS.COM

For Adam and Wilma

CONTENTS

FOREWORD

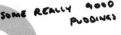

SOME REALLY GOOD PUDDINGS

FOREWORD

FOREWORD

The ridiculousness of writing a memoir aged twenty-six is not lost on me. It's obviously a complete joke. I'm neither a politician, rock star or sportsperson – I'm just a gobby little shit with a lot of things to say who has managed to wangle an editor who has the unenviable job of making it readable.

It is a truly human desire to make stories out of the events that befall us. We all simply want to understand, to come to some sort of conclusion, to weave what is in reality a thousand loose threads into a tapestry of meaning. We are desperate to take the chaos of existence and turn it into something beautiful and full of substance. Ultimately, we will fail. Life is not a pretty throw from Urban Outfitters with a general thrust and message. Life is screaming pain and confusion with a few moments of respite and, if you're lucky, a couple of really good puddings. I have embarked on an impossible task and all I can hope is that you enjoy reading this as much as I have enjoyed writing it.

I should address why this is a memoir. I could have written a thinly veiled autobiographical fictional novel. One garners more respect for that, I think. But it is my duty to tell my truth and label it as such. Also, you don't get an advance for fiction you haven't written and I like to get my money upfront.

I have spent much time debating internally late at night when I would much rather be sleeping. I have wrestled over what events I would put in this book. Should I include my sexual awakening in gory detail (Keanu Reeves in *Bill and Ted*)? Should I include a series of heartbreaks from friends, lovers and family members? Do I write about my father's adoption? Do I write about the long line of child abuse that ends with my mother? (This is my next project, so please be patient.) What is mine to tell? All of these things are intrinsic to me, my life and my identity. They are the building blocks of who I am.

But in this instance, I am going to be a tease and not talk about those things at all. This book contains a deep dive into my experiences with education, creativity and neurodiversity. My story is that after an unconventional school route I found myself, against the odds, studying at one of the most prestigious universities in the world. But after failing some exams at the University of Oxford, I was diagnosed with dyslexia and dyspraxia. Not only did I have no clue what those words meant, I had no idea that they could be applied to me. This book is an exploration of that journey and an attempt to understand how on earth I could have slipped through the gaps for the first twenty years of my life.

With this very specific theme, I ought to clarify a few things. Specific Learning Difficulties (SpLDs) is the general name for a family of differences in learning. It is basically about how the brain processes the world around it. We all have different cognitive profiles, which is to say we each have strengths and weaknesses, but SpLDs are diagnosed by looking at the disparity in those strengths and weaknesses. That is to say: the focus is on the gap.

There are many ways in which we can be neuro-divergent: Autism/ASD, Dyslexia, Dyspraxia, Tourette's, Anxiety, ADD/ADHD, Dyscalculia, Dysgraphia, Developmental Language Disorder, to name a handful. I am not going to write long and scientific definitions of each of these; you have Google and there are educational psychologists and individuals with PhD brains who would be horrified by my bastardisation of these complex subjects. I deal in stories and jokes and feelings. But here is my very brief attempt at explaining the SpLDs that feature in this book:

- *Dyslexia:* language and words are tricky and slippy. Don't ask us to spell.

- *Dyspraxia:* space and time is weird. We fall over and have trouble organising.

- *ADHD:* if it's boring we need to find something more interesting, and when we do we have laser focus.

- *Autism:* feelings, sounds and the environment can be very intense and hard to translate.

In other words, SpLDs make us see and experience the world in a very different way. This means that we have an incredible arsenal of strengths which include: compassion, creativity, originality and resilience.

Oh, and some names have been changed to protect the guilty (in my eyes) and the innocent (theirs). Everything I have written is true, or at least I believe it is, and so surely that is even more telling than anything else. This is what happened as far as I'm concerned; if you think differently – write your own book.

CHAPTER 1

BEING

My name is spelt wrong, so what chance did I have? Really, my parents were asking for a dyslexic child. And they did it on purpose. My father hadn't got pissed before he went down the baby registry and then forgot what name they'd decided. It's not that there's an ink smudge on the birth certificate and that now has metamorphosed into my name. No, it was an active decision that my name should be spelt wrong.

Kaiya is usually spelt K-A-Y-A (according to Bob Marley), but my young hippy parents (see: naming your child after a Bob Marley song) weren't so sure that the numerology of the original spelling was quite good enough for their first progeny. Numerology is a way of placing numerical values on letters which can then be simplified down to a value between one and nine and thus divining what sort of person you might be in the future. Adding an 'i' realigned my stars and gave me a better personality. It made sure I was the sweet baby child I turned out to be. Without that 'i', the doctor who delivered me wouldn't have proclaimed I was the most beautiful newborn he'd ever seen (not bragging – just what happened). Without the 'i', I wouldn't have been the toddler that demanded cups of tea upon waking up every morning. I always slept between my parents and started each day with a cup of sweet milky tea in a little mug with The Lowly Worm on. It was chipped and reassembled and glued because I managed to drop it but was uninterested in any other china. Without the 'i', I wouldn't have insisted that my hair, too, should be shaved off when my dad cut off his Jesus locks and my mum decided to rock the skinhead. They're not spiritual nuts, I swear, despite the head shaving and the occasional kaftan. But as my mum says about the whole numerology thing: *why risk it?*

The surname Stone is significant too. My parents both have maiden names which means that when they got married they both changed their surnames. Very progressive, I know. They only got married because they wanted money from their parents to go travelling. They did the deed in Wandsworth, the epicentre of romance, and no members of their families were present. So it made it less awkward when they decided to scrap their surnames – Slater and Aldridge.

They had chosen to start again: new family; new name. My mum, not concerned with the years of schoolchildren shouting *Wilmaaaa*, mimicking Fred Flintstone, saw no potential issues with the new name Stone. The real crime is, of course, that they missed the opportunity to smash their two surnames together and begin the new dynasty. Long live the Slaldridges!

Instead, the Stone family came into being on 3 September 1992 after they picked a new name out of a hat. I like to think they picked it in allusion to the funk kings (Sly and the Family Stone) and British icons (the Stone Roses and the Rolling Stones).

I'm fairly certain that had I been Kaya Slaldridge, I'd be able to spell, play a musical instrument and hold down a real job. Kaya Slaldridge would have met a lovely boy, maybe called Timothy King, and she'd have had a white wedding and changed her surname. She'd smile politely while everyone joked that she should start her own canoeing business. One day she would have snapped, aged fifty-two, and kicked the dog in front of the family. Her children would look at her in disgust and she would go and sit in the pantry and wonder why, oh why, hadn't her parents just put a little 'i' into her name. *Then maybe*, Kaya Slaldridge would wonder, *could I have been a little more selfish?*

But, alas, the power of names has spoken and I am Kaiya Stone. For that I can only apologise.

And I was an accident. My parents, in their early

twenties, had headed off to India, their pockets filled with cash that their own parents would have preferred to have been spent on a ceremony and subpar buffet. Instead, my mum splashed out on some prescription sunglasses so she could finally see and they headed across the world for a year of adventure. Before leaving, Wilma Stone wished to the universe that the trip would change her life. Three months later, she was pregnant with me – not exactly what she had meant. Yet it certainly changed their lives. They had to come back to the UK and as they did my mum swore that having children wouldn't stop her travelling. But really, who aged twenty-two and twenty-four is ready to look after another adult in a long-term relationship commitment, let alone be wholly responsible for a baby?

I'm twenty-six now and I baulk at the idea of this level of obligation, of dedication for another. It's a small miracle that I'm childless, not because I'm having lots of unprotected sex with men, but because I'm the first generation of women in my family on both sides to still be childless at this ripe old age. Maybe we're very fertile, irresponsible or, more likely, Sex-Ed left much to be desired for many young people. My dad was conceived when my Granny Jayne, aged sixteen, lost her virginity in a *shuffle* in a tent. She once told me she didn't even know she was having sex, which is the most scathing post-coital review I've ever heard.

So, I guess my conception was not completely out of the blue. Remember, use a condom, kids, else you might have to end your year-long honeymoon really early, return home and spend your early twenties living in poverty as you scrape together nappy money with loose change from down the back of the sofa.

I was born with my eyes open. I think that's quite symbolic and, more than that, terrifying. I think labour was horrible. I don't remember it but I definitely have lots of residual trauma from being squeezed out of the birthing canal. I know it must have been really horrific for my mother because she had her own mum there. That's who told me I was born with my eyes open. The midwife must have had to hide her horror as I slid out wide-eyed and flipping her the Vs.

From the very beginning, the three of us were a team. I slept on my dad's chest or in the middle of the bed between the pair of them. It gave me great access to tit, something that I still try to maintain in adult life. I have heard that apparently sharing a bed is very dangerous for babies, but I must say I have the most healthy attachment issues of all my friends and I credit this to having breast milk on demand. And this is why I am an entirely functional adult with absolutely no co-dependency issues at all.

My parents' main childrearing technique was to do the opposite of their own upbringings and to build their lives around what I needed, which is pretty fucking radical. They have always built castles around me, have surrendered any of their own ambitions for my wellbeing and fanned the fire in my chest. My parents were always around, poor but always present. In my child's eyes they were never not making: art, clothes, food, change. I was surrounded by the potency of truthful creation. Dad was writing novels, being put on waiting lists only to remain unpublished. Mum was tackling generational trauma and the legal system (an important story for another, but soon approaching, time). But, ultimately, they were young fighting artists on the dole with a tiny baby. It's not romantic, it's shit. They had no clue but they were just trying their best.

They have never insisted I call them 'Mum' and 'Dad', in fact it is very odd typing this out, referring to them as what feels like their drag names. To me, they are Wizzy and Adoo, affectionate bastardisations of their names.

I was raised in a bubble of alternative parenting. For example, as stoners, Wizzy and Adoo were fond of a soap opera. All the classics: *EastEnders*, *Corrie*, *Neighbours*. But when they realised that my tiny baby brain was in fact just a sponge and they caught me singing along with the classic intro music to *Coronation Street* before I could even speak, they jettisoned the telly straight out of my life. I would remain TV-less until my third year of university, where I discovered a passion for shit telly. These days, *Pointless* followed by *The Simpsons* on a weekday feels like I'm catching up on missed hours. Nothing makes me happier than a short sharp shock of a reality dating show. It reminds me that most people are stuck in loveless relationships of convenience just wanting to get to the 'happiest day of their life' as quick as they can so they can stop trying and slide into the abyss of FOREVER with a man named Dave. But then again, I am a hopeless romantic.

But without telly how on earth does one parent? Their solution was the introduction of the most important institution of my life: the Library. Twice a week my mum would go with me and we would pick a pile of books to read. This tradition continued through my entire childhood.

Much to their horror, I was a big fan of princesses and pink. When I started preschool, they let me pick my own lunchbox. Barbie. *Are you sure?* they asked. *Wouldn't you prefer this cool robot one, or one with a puppy, or this one with a lady scientist who runs a feminist mobile library in her spare time?* Nope, my heart was set on the pink and sparkly. Now, my parents keep their word. Not once in my memory have they ever let me down or lied to me (or they're excellent at hypnosis and I have no recollection of a myriad of traumatic disappointments), so they got me the lunchbox. But when we got home, we all sat

round putting stickers over Barbie's petite sculpted body with her pointy breasts and little stumpy feet. Everyone was happy and much to their relief I grew out of pink and glitter.

I was involved in all aspects of family living. We all had dinner together, slept in the same room and shared baths. They really pushed this ethos when they let me decide whether or not I wanted to remain an only child. I was keen to play the part of big sister, a role I have worn with righteous pride since they asked me the question. Obviously, I was not involved in the actual creation of my little brother – but I was there at his birth.

Casius Stone was a home birth. I was supposed to be too, but after thirty hours of labour my mum, never one to refuse drugs, had opted (read: demanded loudly) to go to hospital and have an epidural. Second time round, the hippy home birth was successful. While my mum was panting and doing all the hard work on the living room floor, Adoo and I were lying in bed waiting. The red numbers on the digital clock/radio glowed in the dark while we lay listening to Classic FM. That night was so exciting and it's my earliest memory. Everything earlier than this is mythology. All the other things are stories I've been told and heard for many years. But that moment of anticipation is my first twinkling of consciousness. Although I was two and a half, I knew that everything was about to change and it would be a great thing, plus I would get to be a big sister. I knew I would love him and I did.

I cut Casius's umbilical cord. With hindsight, I'm not sure how responsible it is letting a two-and-a-half-year-old scissor their way through sinew, but luckily the leg grew back. Later, I sat on the sofa in my pyjamas holding Cas, staring at the squished pinkness. It struck me, a thought of 'this-is-the-most-important-thing-in-the-world-and-I-will-die-for-this-baby', which is pretty intense, especially for a toddler. But I am nothing if not consistent.

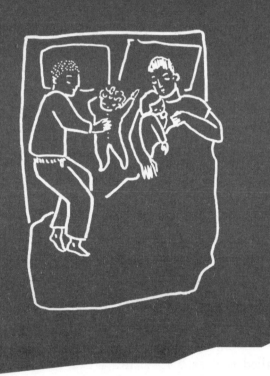

So then there was four, like the Beatles except two of us were children and there was only slightly less sitar. We had been living in Brighton when things began to change. Wizzy wanted to travel and go somewhere new. And my dad's book was dropped off the waiting list so the big break he'd been waiting for went up in smoke. He had to get a Proper Job™. My mum had an uncle and aunt in Cape Town and my dad got a position in advertising over there. So the fab four were going on tour.

I had been raring to get to school from the very beginning of my existence. My granny had got me an elasticated school tie that I would wear as a permanent accessory. I would longingly stare at older kids in the playgrounds of the schools we would pass on the way to Iceland to pick up frozen mince. So when we arrived in Cape Town, I was hyped to start at my first educational institution.

My parents, of course, picked out the school in Cape Town with the same values they had raised me with. It was about as alternative as you would expect for any place called the Children's Studio. It was a very traditional Montessori school, which means mixed-age classes, lots of creativity and a super-liberal schooling system. Everything was taught via the means of sand, pouring and cuddling trees. It was the sort of school where you called the teachers by their first names. Wizzy had looked round when we first arrived in the country and saw these wax crayon and food colouring paintings done by the kids, a signature style overseen by the wondrous Alex Mamacos (who would go on to be a beloved family friend). She decided that's the sort of school she wanted to send her kids to.

There weren't huge numbers of rules at the Children's Studio – just the usual love and kindness ones. They were fascists for peace and understanding. Oh, and you weren't allowed to play as characters from TV or film. So if you were caught pretending to be Spiderman or a Disney Princess, you would be told off for not having enough imagination because we ought to be inventing our own characters. I liked this rule because we didn't have a telly so it meant I didn't have to fake knowledge on the current affairs in cartoons. The other kids would quietly try to play superheroes or Power Rangers. But the pew-pewing and singing of theme tunes tended to give them away. Occasionally some young Einstein would claim that they were in fact playing the book version of Inspector Gadget. Ingenious.

At school, we traded songs. I taught them the rainbow song (which is fundamentally flawed because have you ever drawn a rainbow out in the order red and yellow and pink and green? – rank) and in exchange they taught me political chants. *My body's my body, nobody's body but mine, you've got your own body so let me have mine.*

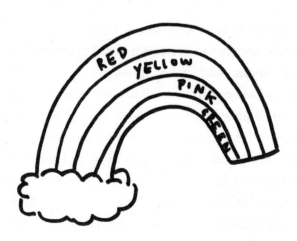

My school was full of kids from all sorts of backgrounds and there were other international children too. My best friend was Thandiwe, or P as she was known back then. Her mum, Alex, was best friends with my parents and not just because of the paintings. We all went up to this house Alex's family owned in the middle of nowhere, De Tois Kluff. On the drive up, there were herds of wild zebra. At the house, there was no electricity or plumbing but a full collection of Asterix books. Me, Thandi and Cas played for hours in the river naked. My other friend in school was a Spanish girl whose parents were doctors and her baby brother I thought was called Avocado (now I realise his name must have been Ricardo). I watched her do flamenco in awe with her tiny castanets. All these little childhood interactions made me realise how much breadth there could be in people's existences.

I remember a lot of this time even though some of my friends say they can't remember anything until they were about nine. We'd moved country in 1997 when I was four and this new home felt very different from Leeds and windy Brighton where we had been living before. The things that I remember sound like the made-up imaginings of a seven-year-old but were a normal part of life in Cape Town. I remember the dassies, these little mountain dwelling rodent-y things that pooed Maltesers. Or the penguins sprayed pink that lived on the beach even when the sun was beating down. The Cape Town we arrived in was at a time of hope – Madiba was president. As far as possible for a little kid, I knew about apartheid but it was hard to see whether it had really ended. Perhaps because it was new, I couldn't help but see how glaringly obvious the divide was. Children are preoccupied with fairness and I was certain that this was not fair. There were two types of houses: the fortresses with bars on the windows and doors and guard dogs that were racist; or the patchwork houses made of metal and cardboard lining the motorways. Wealth and poverty sliced up this new country.

We lived in a bungalow, which felt exotic for its lack of stairs. The garden had a tree with a platform built onto it, we had two cats that used to visit us, it even had its own little playground and you could see Table Mountain from the kitchen window. There was a big wall which I could climb and there was a boy my age who lived on the other side who was my friend. Well, he was, until his parents caught my brother chasing me with a knife one morning when my parents had been out of the room for a moment. But the real nail in the coffin for the relationship was my parents catching his dad using the n word.

Part of the reason the Cape Town chapter of my childhood felt like it was full of imaginings was because I'd moved halfway round the world but also it was because everyone around me was making literal magic happen. At school, there was this weekly cake raffle where every Friday a name would be pulled out of a hat and you got to take home a cake. Then the next week you'd have to bring in the prize cake. To me the only lottery worth winning involves taking home a cake. I pulled out the dream ticket twice, and the best bit was always getting to make the next prize and feeling proud when people really wanted to win it.

The first masterpiece that my mum and I made (mainly her) was a swiss-roll steam train. She bought the cake pre-made and we covered the whole thing in twinkly Jelly Tot jewels. There were chocolate button rivets and Kit Kat pistons. I don't want to blow our own trumpet but it was a feat of edible engineering and parental ingeniousness that involved zero baking and maximum effect. I remember everyone, including my little brother, looking in wonder at this cake as I processed it in on the Friday morning and placed it in the school kitchen to await the Fates to allocate who would get to be the proud owner of such a treat.

Wizzy got a phone call from the school that afternoon. Casius, all angelic with his golden curls, had snuck into the kitchen somehow, presumably SAS-style, shuffling under the shutter. He'd pulled a chair to the table and climbed up. Now, here was the truly ingenious bit. He had eaten the front cylinder of the choccy locomotive, managing to leave the back untouched. But to ensure he wasn't caught, he didn't use his hands. Instead, he must have laid on his belly and chomped away like a snake disguised as a cherub. After gorging on the prize, he settled down to hibernate like any full predator would. A teacher found him napping, I'm presuming with an angelic smile on his cakey mouth, on the table. This was the fatal flaw in his otherwise perfectly executed crime. Wizzy had to go into school, chop the driver's carriage down a bit, whack on a few more sweets, and no one was any the wiser. Cas had gotten to eat the cake he'd seen being made in our kitchen and I got to still give the raffle winner the best cake ever made, albeit a bit shorter than it had been.

This is pretty symbolic of my whole time in Cape Town: weird traditions and free-flowing kindness. My wild-eyed brother wasn't told off because he wasn't naughty, he was excited and no harm was done. I wasn't bothered because it didn't matter and I thought Cas was funny and he was my little brother. For the sake of the narrative arc, I see these as the idyllic years of my childhood; a time where I mostly believed anything was possible.

One morning, I woke up and told everyone it was my birthday on a day that was not in any way my birthday. I played birthdays in the garden and made myself a cake in the sandpit we had. Then Cas and I played some proto-computer games. Ones where we

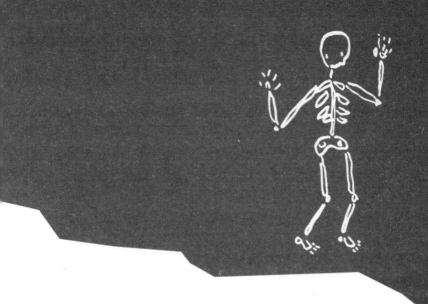

clicked on illustrations and little Easter-egg animations would jump up and sing 'Dem bones'. While we were immersed in the most advanced feats of child entertainment, my parents went to work. After the gaming session, Cas and I left my dad's computer to find a birthday party. Wizzy and Adoo had baked me a real cake and strung up balloons. We all sang happy birthday. Miracles happened and the world felt magic.

In this magic world I was taught the most important thing a child can learn – to love yourself. It sounds cheesy but it's something that I can't help be incredibly thankful for. I was at a school where I was told I was great and I had parents who were fun and loving. I didn't know what would happen in the world, I certainly knew that society was unfair and cruel, but I also knew that unexpected unimaginable wonderful things happened too. I learnt to be kind to myself and others.

At this point, I also began to have my first understandings of mortality and began to obsessively worry about death. More specifically, I became obsessed with suffocating on my own tongue. Something had clicked in my head and I realised that I could die at any moment, life was fragile. I had, however, pinpointed the most likely cause of my death – my traitorous little tongue. I was often found holding onto it in case that little bit of skin snapped and my wet pink mouth muscle wriggled down my throat. The fear of mortality had manifested and has sat with me ever since.

I'm still pretty existential. There is a tension between the confident, cocky and joyful Kaiya and the parts of me who are terrified and full of doubt. I have these waves of panic and worry. I lie in bed and feel so tiny and startled by the enormity of being alive. It's a very specific fear – it stems from wondering *why can we think? What is the point of being alive when we will so quickly, certainly and suddenly disappear forever?* Even as a tiny child, I had some innate understanding that this was 'it', there was no heaven, there was no afterwards, just the right here and the right now. That is a lot of quite heavy and weighty thoughts for a five-year-old, it's a lot for a twenty-six-year-old. So, to deal with all of that I just held my tongue (literally).

My parents tried to soothe my anxious mind. They assured me that only people with epilepsy could swallow their tongues.

But maybe I have epilepsy?

No you don't. You'd know.

What is epilepsy?

It's when you shake and have fits. Sometimes it's triggered by flashing lights.

After that conversation, I became worried about blinking too quick in the light in case that caused me to see flashing lights. At Christmas we went round the shops to get food for the traditional big turkey dinner. I bit firmly onto my tongue all the way round the South African equivalent of Tesco. My granny, who had come over to visit and must have been freaking out that her granddaughter had changed quite drastically with the move halfway across the world, kept asking me why I was holding my tongue, which is not something I have ever been good at in the metaphorical sense. I couldn't get her to understand that if I stopped I risked certain death. I was not going to fall into the trap of unclenching my teeth to explain and then the bit of skin would snap and then I'd choke and die and Granny wouldn't be very happy after that, would she? Christmas would be ruined.[1]

All the neuroses cumulated into one big incident, when I woke up and I was trembling – like little shivers in my hands. Tiny tremors. The more I panicked the bigger I shook. I ran into my parents' bedroom screaming that I was swallowing my tongue and desperately trying to keep a hold of it while speaking. They sat me down and finally explained that epilepsy wasn't something that just happens. After that morning, I stopped holding my tongue but the chasm of consciousness remains a source of great discomfort. I cannot forget that this will all end soon. (Note to self: fridge magnet idea, Life is Loss.)

Something that coincided with all this was that I kept asking what the meaning of life was. I'm sure my

---

1   Apparently my granny didn't visit us in South Africa, so I think I must have relocated this incident to a different country, but the memory still stands. Sorry for being an unreliable narrator. Try not to be too gullible.

parents were wishing I would ask what most six-year-olds ask: things like who would win in a fight between a bear with a machine gun or an octopus with eight throwing daggers. The answer they always gave was *love*, and I was like – *yeah, duh*.

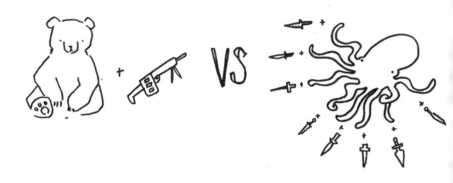

One day I managed to get an alternative response. We had a treasure hunt with our friends Alex and Thandiwe in the woods where I found this little doll. Her little embroidered face seemed so real, but did she have consciousness? I could imagine an inner world for her but that was from my brain. All evidence pointed that she was an inanimate object. Why wasn't I an inanimate object? Why could I even think of such a terrifying question? This triggered my penchant for philosophy once more and I asked again what the meaning of life was. The adults looked at each other and began to discuss all the potential answers. After a couple of minutes they agreed on an Official Line: the most important thing to know was to *know who you are*. Again, I was pretty certain I had that one worked out. I was Kaiya Stone and I loved lots, so I'd got life sorted and as long as I didn't choke on my tongue, I'd be fine. I wish I was still this certain.

CHAPTER 2

LEARNING

Just as I was about to evolve into a Dolphin, what they called the eldest students in my hippy-bippy school in Cape Town, we moved to America. And just like that my one chance to be a clever animal went up in smoke. My dad had been offered another advertising job and it was more money and more travel. So we packed all our things in boxes, gave lots of toys away and waved goodbye to Table Mountain.

That first night we arrived was Halloween 2000. Nana and Beardie, my dad's (adoptive) parents, had given me and Cas weird masks made from that material people wrap fancy fruit in. Mine was a green witch with a wart on her nose and Cas rocked a very disturbing image of Frankenstein's monster. Though, of course, then I would have said he was just Frankenstein because I was eight and hadn't read Shelley yet. But we all know what someone means when they say it – it's just snobbery to point it out.

We went out trick-or-treating in a new country, with our subpar costumes, and it was the very beginning of the culture shock. I was excited for the adventure. But I had no idea what a weird and uncomfortable thing it can be to throw yourself into an unfamiliar place. We came back laden with new foreign sweets; sacks full. I'd never seen, let alone owned, this amount of *candy*. This was my introduction into the OTT nature of the Yanks. Every house was huge and dressed up like a theatre set, with cobwebs and ghouls and lights. Then everyone made such loud and emphatic noises when Casius and I told them it was our first day in America. There's nothing more terrifying to Americans than a new wave of immigration. And there's nothing like being the new kid to claim your own body weight in sugar from strangers.

The first thing we noticed as we poured out our hauls onto the floor of our new pad was that the sweets were so weird. So much chocolate and peanut butter combined. Then brightly coloured sugar-flavoured shapes, Candy Corn. Little silver-foil-covered turds, Hershey's Kisses. Weird shrink-wrapped cakes with creme fillings. Everything had to be spelt wrong because it wasn't really chocolate or really cream or really cake. It was a trademarked approximation of food. We were there at the height of the fake food gastronomic innovation. The era of Oreos that turned milk blue when you dunked them, 3D Doritos (although not as exciting as they sound) and Heinz deciding that red ketchup was a thing of the past with their EZ Squirt in mouth-watering shades of green or purple. I can't help but think such feats of engineering would have been better spent in pioneering affordable healthcare, but let's not forget this was America after all. Freedom tastes delicious.

I joined first grade in Bedford Village Elementary. My teacher was called Mrs Zwick and I liked her a lot. She had a big cloud of curly black hair and smiling eyes. Mrs Zwick took a shine to me, warmly welcoming me into her classroom and encouraging her pupils to do the same. American school was weird. There were less child-height shelves and trays and a whole lot more injections, sticker collecting and public rituals with implicit ceremonies that everyone else understood. Take Valentine's Day, for example, when you were expected to give chocolate to everyone, even though you're eight years old and you don't fancy any of them. I didn't know any of these unsaid rules. So I began being an outsider. A state I've either sat in or thought I sat in for most of my life.

There were a lot of reasons for me not to fit in here. Firstly, the little hamlet we lived in had a community of just 1,724 (according to the census they held in 2000, the year we moved there), so everyone noticed the one new girl with the South African accent. The other thing was that the median income for a household there appeared to be something along the lines of the pool of gold Scrooge McDuck nosedives into.

Now, to put this into context, we were living in someone's outhouse and to use my mother's choice phrase *we didn't have a pot to piss in*. Admittedly, rich families' sheds are still pretty nice as it goes, but it was a whole different world. I would go round other kid's houses and they would have a separate room to put all their once-touched toys in and then I'd go home to a shared mattress on the floor (and food and clothes, just no bed frame). The real difference, however, was that I saw my parents. These kids were spoilt brats, given stuff because no one was around apart from some much-abused nanny, and Mommy and Daddy felt guilty.

School brings all of these things into a very particular focus:

Oh my god, you've never heard Britney Spears before?!

What a cute little accent!

So what sort of car does your dad have? And your mom? Only ONE car?

What do you mean you don't have a nanny?

Mainly it wasn't bad. I was exciting and new and different so I made friends. I learnt quickly that I needed to have some commodities to be taken seriously. That particular year the currency was stickers. I had a sticker book with puppies on and inside I collected velvety Dalmatians, shiny butterfly and cartoon characters I didn't know (still no telly). We would trade and swap and gift. The greatest of all were oilies. These squishy stickers with what looked like a BP oil spill in them. The colours changed and swirled when you pushed down on them. You would have to trade something like four shinys and five velvets for one of those bad boys. Once I had some currency, I could build some social relationships.

From these friendships my world expanded once again. I wasn't Jewish nor had I ever met anyone who was before, so I learnt about Hanukkah. I learnt about the Disney Channel and brands. I learnt that certain music was the right thing to listen to and certain films were must-see. This was a million miles from a school which wouldn't allow mention of Spiderman.

But one of the weirder things was that I'd missed a school year – sort of. In the US of A, you start kindergarten at four and start reading, writing and filing tax returns. But I'd come from a different system where I'd been taught I'd do all that letters and numbers stuff after I'd had some fun with pouring and touching sand.

I found myself lost. I simply couldn't do what
everyone else could; I was struggling. I'm not sure
I realised that I was so behind. I went to the toilet
a lot. I would wander down the corridors and sit in
the cubicle until a teacher came to find me.
I remember being like 'I was just having a
poo' when they asked me if I was OK in that
patronising American voice. I don't know why
I lied and I don't remember consciously not wanting
to be in class. At that point in my life the teachers
thought that maybe I had a learning difficulty. But I
had also missed kindergarten... I could just be very
behind because I had gone between two different
systems. Either way, their solution was to give me one-
on-one tutoring. Each day I did an hour with a woman
whose name I can't remember. She can't have been that
important – she only taught me to write.

The way she taught me was simple. I just had to write one sentence a day. We'd discuss it, settle on the sentence and then began the arduous, torturous task of putting pencil to page.

When I think about writers and writer's block, I think about little Kaiya clutching onto her pencil as hard as she could, face levitating only inches from the page as she struggled to squeeze out a sentence. Trying to write when you can't is like trying to milk a stone or squeeze out a particularly solid shit. Everything is an obstacle and the prospect seems impossible. You look at the blank page and wonder how on earth I can put what I'm thinking into the symbols everyone else understands. Honestly, it's a miracle that anyone can write.

Firstly, you have to pick up the writing implement. In the early days, it'll be a pencil or a crayon maybe. Then you have to navigate how you hold the bloody thing. Your hand swerves round it trying to work out what the best angle to pick it up is. Initially, you want to curl your whole little fist around it, punching it into the page, but some well-meaning middle-aged woman with 'jazzy' earrings will soon correct your form. You have to hold it in the most complex pinching gymnastic contortion. When you finally sort that you hold onto the position for dear life with a white-knuckle grip.

And then there's spelling or working out what image you have to put on the page and the sound that it chimes. So you have to sound out each bit of the word, finding its corresponding letter. Some are easy, the ssss of a slithering snake and a letter that curls like an adder. But vowels are nearly impossible to distinguish – not that you know what a vowel is – so you just guess one between a e o and hope you're lucky.

Then comes the mark-making. Each word is made up of letters. Each letter is made up of lines. You're supposed to do the lines in a certain order, a certain size and sitting on the blue line on the page. If you can see the image in your mind, your trembling hand can't quite mimic it. You try to copy the examples but yours are big, wobbly and nothing like the neat printing of teacher.

It is no wonder that one day I went into the special room for kids that needed extra help, defiance running through my veins. I sat down with crossed arms and scowling.

I don't want to write a sentence today.

It was all too much effort. I knew that she couldn't make me, or could she? Well, I guess we would find out. She looked at me smiling, her head cocked.

Well, why don't you write that down?

It hit me like a sack of bricks. What she'd just suggested was the greatest idea ever held by man. It was true rebellion, defiance in its finest form, it was political graffiti! To write that I didn't want to write. It would be permanent. That moment was a realisation that I could write anything. It didn't have to be 'I like cats' and 'today I will go swimming'. It could be so much more.

i doht waht
to rit senths todai

Took me an hour to scrawl it out but at the end I felt full of dissent and power. I'd won that battle. At its best that's how it feels when I write as an adult. I think because of how many hurdles it takes just to put something down on paper sometimes, it becomes freeing. The struggle to write it down means that I can't be too harsh about what I am writing about.

After that little incident, my nameless teacher told

me that I was going to grow up to be a writer. Having read and spoken to other people with learning difficulties, this strikes me as extraordinary. I often think about why on earth she said that. Was it simply to encourage me or was it because I was? I was told that I should consider a career doing a lot of reading and writing even though at that time I couldn't objectively do those things very well at all. So naturally I learnt to write because why wouldn't I have? I was going to be a writer. Someone older and cleverer than me told me that I was. Let's all be thankful she hadn't said firefighter or doctor, else I'd be playing with other people's lives not just my own.

So my future was set out for me. I would sit in a room full of books and audio books and comics and write with fancy pens on coloured paper and my stories would be the story equivalents of having cream and ice cream on jelly. It wouldn't matter that I wasn't American or that I didn't understand Valentine's Day or Independence Day or that I made up the pledge of allegiance every single morning.

That incident gave me a mantra, which I'm afraid to say I have used ever since: *It's all just material*. From the age of seven, when things happened to me that made me sad or angry I would shuffle it into a part of my brain and tell myself that it was just something to write about. I'm not entirely convinced it's the best method of coping with suffering, but it is fruitful.

So I went to school every day on a yellow school bus. I was living the American dream: bagel boats for lunch. (If memory serves, they were just sandwiches with bagel as the bread. In no way aquatic.)

While writing remained a struggle, books were a steadfast place of refuge. I love reading and I always have. I just absolutely love stories, all sorts of stories. It started with those trips to the library. We'd pick the books my parents would read to me before bed. All the heavy hitters – *Handa's Surprise*, *The Rainbow Fish*, that one about the kid who cuts their knee. Then it was Topsy and Tim and Paddington and Tintin. And Roald Dahl – I know everyone agrees – but bloody hell – he's great. He had made-up words and told us stories of real-life magic and evil adults. There were sweets and farts and flying and lawbreaking – a child's dream and a normal weekend for me (then and now).

Then, of course, it was Harry Potter. We lived in America from 2000 to 2001 and obviously the newest book fad had hit the world hard. My mum read them to me and I was completely taken over. I used to beg, beg, beg please one more chapter. She used to go hoarse from reading aloud for hours. The solution to this was audiobooks.

For my fifth birthday I had received a cassette player. It was a black Casio with a little handle you could pull out so you could, as I did, carry it around like a handbag, going about your daily tasks and be soundtracked wherever you went. I still have it: it was my most prized possession for many years and it would be a real disservice to get rid of it even if it is a phased-out bit of technology. I'm still waiting for the cassette renaissance, if vinyl had it so will rewinding tapes and making mixtapes off the radio.

I spent much of my early childhood listening to the same stories on repeat. It allowed me to access stories that, if I had been left solely to my reading ability, I would never have been able to read, like *Little Women* for example. This allowed my brain to begin to wrestle with odd vocabulary and old-fashioned sentence structures that if I had seen them on the page I would have run a mile.

I would turn out the light and listen till I fell asleep. We borrowed tapes from the library and (don't grass on us) record our own cassettes off them. I'd watch the wheels go round and round. The whir of the cassette was as important a part of it as the narrator. The noise of analogue and having to wind in streams of loose tape with a pencil just built a stronger emotional experience with the story. Some of those voices are so closely knitted to my childhood and certain actors feel like close family members. Sandi Toksvig will always be Wilma the dumpy witch from *Wilma's Wicked Revenge* and no number of Radio 4 comedy panel shows will undermine that. I will also fight anyone to the death who disagrees that Jim Dale is the ultimate voice of Harry Potter.

I have always been allowed to read anything. No books have been out of bounds. My parents always believed that I would self-censor. They were right. I would just stop reading books that got too scary. There were cassettes that I would miss out. In my set for

Goodnight Mr Tom I would always miss out the horrifying bits; side A on the third tape was only played once. The self-censoring thing worked because often adult books are quite tricky for kids to read and generally they are pretty dull.

They were stricter with TV and films. With books you have to understand the words. Then imagine things. Your limit is your imagination and your own set of references. Books work with the readers acting as film directors. The words trigger images and we create pictures that chime into our own personal worlds. Whereas films have already been made. The images are there. I couldn't really imagine a room made of skin until I saw *Jeepers Creepers*. Now I can. I didn't sleep for a solid two weeks after that sleepover when I was thirteen. I get to be in control with books.

I learnt more from books than I ever learnt in school. I guarantee you that. School was all well and good but, even from the beginning, I was aware that I had to take what I was being taught in school with a pinch of salt. For example, soon after we arrived in America, Thanksgiving came round. We started learning about Chris Columbus and the discovery of America. My mum sat me down after school one day. I remember her looking me in the eye.

America existed before colonialism. People lived here before white people. Thanksgiving doesn't acknowledge that. White people came here and we stole and we murdered. We have to be careful what we accept as truth.

This obviously stood in big contrast to the lessons I was being taught in elementary school – of welcoming, of discovery, of the land of free. What can a paper turkey wearing a pilgrim hat teach you? What does marshmallow melted over sweet potato tell children about colonialism? From then I realised that there was more than just one side of the story and, just because a teacher tells you one thing, doesn't make it the whole truth.

My dad got a laptop, a Mac. He needed it for work. It was a huge deal – it had a DVD player. This was the height of technology and it meant we could drive down into town and go to Blockbusters. The first film we watched on the laptop was *Star Wars: A New Hope*. It was obviously a pivotal moment. It's hard to say who I related to more. Earnest Luke with his floppy 1970s hair, Leia a badass princess or Hans in his sexy little leather vest spitting sarcastic lines. In many ways, they are the trinity of my own personality. But more than that, the first time I saw the pink sky with two suns setting with John Williams's score swelling, I realised that I too could feel that longing for something to happen. The blushing oranges lighting up Tatooine was a beacon. A symbol that the huge world was opening up and offering epic stories to me. Dad told me about when he had gone to the preview of *Star*

Wars aged eight. That it was life-changing for him. It felt good to be a part of that legend, too, to have my own version. He explained that *Star Wars* was in fact a Samurai story and that it had all the parts that all ancient myths have. I guess it was my introduction to *The Hero with a Thousand Faces*. I was so fascinated with the idea that this epic, set in the past, and yet also the future, was part of a long tradition of storytelling.

When I wasn't lying about listening to stories, thinking about R2-D2, or feeding our neighbour (a potbellied pig) popcorn, I was thinking a lot. I had continued to wonder who I was and unfortunately hadn't quite grown out of self-reflection. I had received a compilation album of reggae classics for another birthday. I danced innocently around to Musical Youth's 'Pass the Dutchie' and to Dawn Penn's 'You Don't Love Me (No No No)'. I would lie around wondering why Cameron from the other class didn't return my intense feelings (which I only actually felt while listening to that particular song). This is early evidence that I am in fact just an emotional sponge. But one particular track hit me very hard.

My dad was adopted. I had always known Nana and Beardie weren't his biological parents. But my dad had been looking for his birth family for several years. Then along came Jayne and the Boys. My father found his birth mother, who had recently been widowed, and he also found out he had three teenage half-brothers –

Jonny, Andy and Dave.

Now, the third track on my compilation album was Eek-a-Mouse's 'Ganja Smuggling'. It was my dad's favourite but I didn't really know why. But it felt very significant. I was for some reason completely certain that the man singing was my paternal birth grandfather. He sings about his girl, Jayne. I'd just met my new grandmother with the same name, coincidence I think not. More than just that, there was one line about Mummy and Daddy being so poor that we all slept on the floor. I'm paraphrasing but I've already mentioned that my little family shared a mattress on the floor in our American pad. It was all too much for my little head. I held this secret very close to my chest. It was only recently that I realised the absurdity of all this. I was lying awake at night thinking about my long-lost grandfather, the singjay from Kingston. You can't imagine my disappointment when I did eventually meet Micky ten years later when he was an old white guy living in Oxfordshire.

Jayne and the Boys came to visit us in the summer before we moved back to the UK. It was an opportunity to bond with the new family. We went on a big road trip, in two cars, from New York all the way down to Florida. The outward journey took three days. I love epic car journeys. I stared out of windows, at the changing scenery and at the men driving trucks alongside us. I made up stories of who they were and why they were driving. I wondered how many of them were also going on a big holiday with long-lost family. At least three or four of them I concluded. We stopped

for pancakes in diners and slept in motels.

When we arrived, we were staying in a holiday cottage with a pool in a big glass house looking out onto a golf course. This being Florida, we could see 'gators crawling with their jaws snapping as they travelled leisurely across the swampland. This triggered weeks of Steve Irwin impressions from the Boys and my dad. We cannonballed into the pool, we took photos under the water with those special disposable cameras and drank gallons of Doctor Pepper. We went down log flumes and went to all the Orlando parks there were. We went to NASA, but the freeze-dried ice cream ended my short-lived career ambition of being an astronaut. Fun holidays are a good way to start a family, I guess.

What was odd, though, was knowing that at the end of this trip we were moving back to England. The holiday was a flag in our time in America, marking the time as over. We were moving to a world so distant from everything else I remembered. I'd never been to school in Britain, and I had no idea if it would be the same. At Bedford Village Elementary, the facilities were exemplary. They had a school nurse, who when you lost a tooth gave you a special little box to take it home in. They had a little printing press where they turned the students' work into bound colour-illustrated hardback books (even this one you're reading now is black and white!). Each child had a little cubby hole and the school had an internal post system so you could write each other letters. What would I do without Mrs Zwick, who was so warm, and my lady who taught me to write?

We were moving back because we had no money, despite my dad's supposedly fancy job. My mum hated America, she was isolated and her visa didn't allow for her to work. Plus, alongside Adoo's new relationship with his mother, my own mum had to go and help her own family who were in a state of chaos. I accepted this move, sad to be losing what I knew but excited for new possibilities.

So we were moving home, back to Yorkshire.

SPROUTING

CHAPTER 3

SPROUTING

I was born in Leeds. My mum grew up in West Yorkshire and her parents now lived in a place called Morley. Like lots of the towns in this particular bit of the world, it is an ex-industrial zone. It's not a mining town, though of course you're never too far from a mine. In fact the main source of work used to be textiles, but now the role of big employer was up for grabs.

When we moved back to the UK, we had to move in with my maternal grandparents, Granny and Granddad. We had no money. America had not been the financial success my parents had hoped and so the Stones had to return empty-pocketed and reliant on familial generosity. When moving back, I didn't feel sad to leave America but it certainly didn't feel like moving home. I was excited to be much closer to all my family but it was impossible not to feel the waves of deflation radiating from Wizzy and Adoo. This was not at all the life they wanted for us. Living with my grandparents had been a temporary plan which dragged on for two years, much to my parents' horror. They were both living in a state of emergency.

Granny and Granddad had the space; they had bought two Victorian semis when my granddad's entrepreneurship had one (fleeting) successful patch. They knocked down the walls between them to make a double residence, like a Kit Kat. They had five children and enough rooms for everyone. When I think of that building on Westfield Place, I see it sliced open like a doll's house. The house had these long corridors and two sets of stairs for each floor, which really made games of catch very exciting. There were attic rooms and a pair of basements. One was a creepy storage room and the other the children's telly room. There was a grassy sloping back garden with one wall backing onto a Morrisons and a front garden paved in terracotta chess board slabs. The kitchen was bright yellow and there was an Ikea print of Kandinsky's circles. I used to look at it and be reminded of Cape Town; it looked like something one of the kids at the Children's Studio would have made. In the dining room there was a huge table, big enough to fit grandparents, five children, husbands and wives and five grandchildren. We didn't all live there at the same time but almost all of the Aldridges were in the area, in and out.

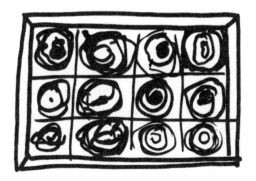

While it had a high emotional cost for my own parents (as it inevitably would, moving back as an adult), living with Granny and Granddad was fun for me and Casius. They are consummate hosts and food is their weapon of choice. They cook big delicious meals. Vats of sweet and sour with huge chunks of pineapple and slabs of their own version of lasagne, Spaghetti Pie. Tatty scones and pancakes and Eccles cakes all whipped up with ease. We all sat round the long table with oil-cloth covering, forming a production line filling and folding spring rolls. After tea (dinner), there was a whole drawer of sweets you could dip into. You were never more than three metres from a Tunnock's caramel wafer or teacake in that house. My belly got round and a sweet tooth was cultivated.

Not only were they great at feeding, my grandparents had Sky (aftermath from Granddad's flash-in-the-pan business success). We went from no telly to 300+ channels overnight. Miracles do happen. The kids' living room was combined with the TV room in the right-hand-side basement. The brown

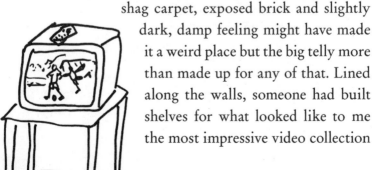

shag carpet, exposed brick and slightly dark, damp feeling might have made it a weird place but the big telly more than made up for any of that. Lined along the walls, someone had built shelves for what looked like to me the most impressive video collection

I'd ever seen. All the Disney films one could wish for and then the classic musicals, *West Side Story* and *My Fair Lady*.

After school we would run down and watch telly for hours. Cas needed more than me. He would wake up at 5 a.m. and sneak into the basement to get in some solid viewing hours of *Digimon* and *Yu-Gi-Oh!*. I much preferred films; I liked the wholeness of the stories. They also didn't just have a video player but on special occasions the whole family would curl up on the multiple sofas in the basement to watch a laserdisc. They had the other original *Star Wars* and so only then in Yorkshire did I get to finish the trilogy. The medium felt perfect, futuristic and yet of the past.

I was still an obsessive story consumer. I listened to my cassettes again and again. But I only had a limited number of them so I had to read more actual books. Michael Morpurgo, Jacqueline Wilson, Anne Fine and my mum's old copies of Enid Blyton books. I'd be put to bed and after I'd heard the responsible adult's steps quieten down, the light would be flicked back on. I would read for a couple of hours and then pad down three flights of carpeted stairs, claiming I couldn't sleep. I don't think anyone believed that I had childhood insomnia.

We had returned to the UK at the end of the summer, so we were just in time to start afresh in the academic year. I was supposed to start second grade in America but here I had to enter into Year 3. Being an August baby, I was the youngest in the year. Not that it really mattered, in a photo taken of my class in an assembly I am a head taller than anyone else. Because there were two primary schools in the area, we got to pick which one we wanted to go to. Either the one which my mum had attended twenty years earlier or the one which my cousins were already at. Having heard stories of my mum being teased and the prospect of pre-made friends, we picked to go to Morley Victoria.

It was a third type of different, nothing like the two schools before. The classes were huge, they had to squeeze me into Miss Hagen's group of thirty-five. The school weren't pleased. I had to wear a uniform for the first time: a little jumper and polo shirt, skirt and shoes. I finally got to look the part. In this school, everyone seemed to be poor and white, just like us. My parents weren't even the youngest and there were a solid handful of us living with grandparents. Most of us were on free school lunches, queuing up for turkey twizzlers, chips and chocolate custard. In many ways it felt like I resembled lots of the other kids, but they didn't see it that way. Obviously the rest of the class hadn't already

lived in two other countries. Most of them didn't have passports. While my voice was an international mishmash, they all had broad Yorkshire voices with an accentuation which made them sound like old men in flat caps. But after flitting about, being the new kid felt normal to me. I was able to talk to anyone and – let's not pretend – I loved the attention. So the first few weeks were fun and exciting.

Because the teachers weren't sure what level I was working on I started in all the bottom ability groups. I had to read all the baby books and prove mesen (which is how you say myself in that particular corner of West Yorkshire). They were impressed, all that extra help I had received in America had made a huge difference. It is not hard to imagine how easily I could have disappeared among the kids who struggled had I not received such targeted help early on. But here, I was no longer behind. I was a very keen, if not always accurate, reader. But writing was a very different thing. I could put together a sentence; well, I think I could. But the problem I had was with spelling and handwriting.

I couldn't really work out how to tell the difference between a b and a d. They looked so similar to me. I knew they made different sounds but I couldn't quite work out a way of discerning which way round they went. In spelling tests, I was stumped by a whole variety of sounds. I would try to get around it by making my letters look like they could be various different things. I would draw the stem of the mystery b/d in the centre and hope the teacher wouldn't notice (they did). But instead of taking this as any particular sign of difficulty with language processing they would just tell me it was weird:

It's so weird, you read so much but it just doesn't correlate with your writing.

It's so weird, you've got such a good vocabulary but you can't spell.

It's so weird, you work hard but...

My mum and I would practise for those spelling tests for hours. Covering and writing. Covering and writing. Repetition. Repetition. Evening after evening. Then it was times tables. I found it all mind-numbingly boring. I just picked up on patterns for both. I noticed the digits for answers in the nine times table added up to nine; that saved me some time. When I asked my mum how to spell words, she would have to write it out to see what 'looked right'. So that's how I learnt to spell, by looking at how words formed on a page, like a picture. I learnt that school had a rogue h in it, I learnt to recognise that because and beautiful had an odd collection of vowels in them. I would recite the mnemonic or the rhyme as I went around the house with a slice of buttery toast in my paw.

So we would just practise for hours, thinking nothing of it. I did it because there wasn't an alternative and I was a relatively compliant student. I liked school and work. I wanted to do well. In many ways, school was easy because I read at home all the time. I had ideas and I liked drawing and making things. At its best, that is what primary school is really.

None of us knew what was normal or what was weird. I was my parents' first kid. My grandparents hadn't exactly been keen on education when it came to their own children. I think that lots of adults have had such a horrific time at school that when it comes to their own children they don't want to even think about it. I heard tales of my granddad hating school, getting beaten and ridiculed – just like Roald Dahl in *Boy,* I thought to myself. People in my family didn't go to university. You did vocational training (my granny had been a nurse) or you left school at sixteen. My uncle Irvin had been doing badly in school and so Granddad had just sent him to Germany to learn the hotel business from a friend of his instead of sitting the equivalent of GCSEs. My mum left school very unceremoniously the moment she could tell the teachers to fuck off. My dad scraped together two O-levels and a BTEC. But they knew from struggling in London, and seeing just who got to make art and be successful, that education was the key. Their children would be different and I loved school, so they would do everything they could to make sure I got to take advantage of learning. At the time, it never felt like any pressure but there is no way to escape that my parents always worked incredibly hard, and they had big ambitions for me. I didn't ever think they were wrong.

There were a few notable instances in my first primary school. We visited Eureka!, a science museum with a raised moving water feature of Archimedes getting into the bath. As he dipped in the bath, water would cascade out. It was a manic day trip: we climbed through huge body parts and put our hands in dark holes and tried to guess their contents. The final exhibit was a kid-size adult world with a bank and mechanics. The supermarket was an M&S, which I thought was very posh. I'd never been in a real one before. The highlight was the system of air tubes which connected all the various parts of the town. We shoved piles of fake cash in what looked to us like clear Pringle cans and screamed as it hoovered our secret messages away. For school trips my dad would make me an extra special packed lunch with a cake bar, chocolate mousse, fruit winders and crisps. I was properly fuelled for the excitement, and this is what I imagined being rich was like.

I reached my personal apex in 2001/2002. There was a general election and the school decided that we would have our own. Each class had to form a political party, make some manifestos and choose leaders. I volunteered myself and gave a speech in front of the whole school, promising a climbing wall and tarmac art. We filled the voting booth and marked Xs on ballots. The count was in and we won. Unfortunately, my politics career was short-lived, but the modular climbing holds are still drilled on the low wall nearly twenty years later.

Then there was the World Cup. Teachers rolled the telly on wheels into the hall and we sat cross-legged on the cold floor in our plimsolls. I watched, wondering what all the fuss was about. We had a sweepstake and I pulled Sweden and Brazil. I cheered on the Swedes and was disappointed to have my favourites knocked out. When Brazil won, I graciously received my prize, a rubber with the country's flag on.

The year ended on another high: Queenie's Golden Jubilee. Fifty years on the throne. The school threw a party and there was bunting everywhere, foreshadowing its terrible resurgence a decade later. But before the godawful Keep Calm posters came to ubiquitous power, my school opened up a competition to design the school's logo to celebrate this great monarchist feat. I won, and my logo was put on fake leather bookmarks that every student got. With hindsight, I wonder where all the money for this memorabilia came from because there didn't seem to be enough money for anything else.

While I have lots of memories of wonderful events, this time was significant for also marking the start of a slow unravelling of my innocence. I began to see the world as a big place, even bigger than just the places I had lived and the people that I had met. I became obsessed about the Holocaust after studying the Second World War and evacuation. It's odd how in primary schools we study this period all cheerfully with talk of baddies and rationing. We sing 'Pack Up Your Troubles' and crawl into bomb shelters. But is it really suitable for eight-year-olds? Especially the obsessive sort who will go on to read about Anne Frank and then how people were rounded up and gassed. I couldn't understand how it happened, the scale of it, and I began to understand how the world was full of potential for real cruelty. While I had recurring nightmares about being smuggled out of Nazi Germany sewn into a mattress, teachers encouraged us to imagine having baths in five inches of water.

I survived my own morbid thoughts by reminding myself that that was in the past. But, one day, I was collected from school by my aunt and she looked funny. The radio was on and there was no music, just talk of planes. At home we sat around the TV in the basement and we saw the second aircraft collide and the towers folding in on themselves and crumple to the ground. It had been my first week in my new school. I had been up to the top of the World Trade Center just before we left America. The height had made my belly tingle and now I knew that no one could stand, looking down on the streets below, like I had just months before. It didn't take much to erase a hundred floors from the skyline. Everything was fragile.

Later came something else new – moments of shame. Unwillingly, I became aware of other people's opinions of me and how that could make me feel hot and sick and small. I began to realise that people didn't like me. I was told that I was odd. We all are really, but I hadn't previously been aware of my own oddity. I just believed that everyone wanted to be my friend, that the baseline of all our interactions was sweet kindness. Like most children, I was preoccupied with justice and fairness. But then came a barrage of comments which undermined that belief. After I had my hair cut for the first time in a hairdressers', I was mocked the next day in school for being excited about having layers. Apparently, I was years behind the rest of the girls.

All the other times I'd had my hair cut by my dad at the kitchen table. He had worked for three days sweeping up hair aged sixteen, thus making him the most qualified parent for this job. So I learnt that a professional haircut with layers was nothing worth speaking about. I was left out of games. I wouldn't be invited to parties. I just couldn't work out what made me so different and worthy of singling out.

Only occasionally were the teachers less cruel. I can't recall the specific words they said to me but what I do remember is the hot flush of embarrassment. I remember exactly where I was sitting each time a comment was made. On the left leg of the horseshoe table. In the back corner under the clock. Focusing on my exercise book. Staring at a poster of times tables in primary colours. Blinking back tears. My mum wrote letters that got no response: *I don't believe humiliation is a suitable technique for educating our children.*

I was OK at following rules. But I would get stuck on certain steps of education. I just couldn't get my pen licence. Firstly, nothing is more ridiculous than

the idea of a pen licence. We let people own animals, have kids and join the army but we don't allow  children to stop writing in pencil and move onto pen without teacher's permission. I watched on longingly as all the lovely nice blonde girls around me with neat cursive got their certificates and moved on to those red Berol handwriting pens. My scrawl couldn't get past the eagle eyes of the teacher. I was left behind with the boys that threw things around the class. It made me feel like shit, like I was shit. I would write in pen at home in secret, certain that if I was caught I would be expelled from school. All I wanted was to be allowed to make permanent marks. Pencil smudges and fades but a biro is forever, as many of my white shirts can attest to.

After my mum went away without us for the first time ever, she brought me back a present: a fountain pen. I couldn't believe it. It was so magical, with its metal nib and cartridges. The clip on the lid was gold

and formed an arrow at its point. I felt like the old lawyer in *The Aristocats* twisting it open and closed to refill the ink. I knew I could write anything with this pen. But just not in school. I was notably upset that I had the greatest weapon in the world but that I had to leave it at home as I left each weekday. My mum asked why I wasn't using it. I wailed that I still didn't have my licence. I had let her down.

Of course, she was having none of that sort of talk from me and sent me off to ask special permission to use it in lessons. The teacher said she would think about it. After two days of deliberation, the licence committee must have decided that if this nine-year-old was that bothered about writing with a pen it was probably easier to just let her. I never did officially get the licence (and it was a beautiful certificate: A5 yellow card, emblazoned with Curlz MT), which proved to me that it was all bullshit.

After a couple of years, we moved out from my grandparents' house, which meant a change of school. Again, I was squeezed into the class. Pushing the rules to let me in, pupil number thirty-six. A class with four Jacks, three Bens and two Ellies but just one Kaiya. One girl made my life hell. She lied, would tell people I spread rumours, she claimed I stole things from her. I kept asking my mum: why doesn't she like me? I haven't done anything to her. Why? At the end of the year, she invited me to her birthday party, an elite affair with only five guests. She cried when I left the class and asked me to stay in contact. It melted my mind. She had just wanted to be my friend all along. People are weird.

In Year 6, in my third and final primary school, as a leavers' present the teachers had a personalised mug made for our year. We all drew ourselves and it was printed on the cup. Most people will be familiar with this – it's usually tea towels – but what ten-year-old has any use for a rag to wipe up surfaces? We got given tiny postage-stamp-sized pieces of paper and were instructed to make our self-portrait snappy. The black pens they gave us were too wide. I tried to capture my distinctive features. My hair was long, like all the girls in my class, so that wouldn't distinguish me at all. But I have a mole above my lip, like Marilyn Monroe or Mutya from the Sugababes. I drew myself and then realised I had to put my name on the picture. I scribbled my name as if it was pouring out of my head. When I handed it in, one classmate pointed out that I looked like a witch. Strike one, I noted. I saw that everyone else had neatly printed their name under their drawing. Strike two. The teacher frowned very slightly when I handed it in. Strike three. I was mortified. Why couldn't I just do things the right way like everyone else? It was another reminder by the world that there was some unmentioned code of being that seemingly had been programmed into everyone else and here I was having to play along when I didn't even know the name of the game. It was frustrating and it made me sad.

Now that mug sits in the family bathroom, full of old toothbrushes that no one is entirely sure who they belong to. When I first got it I spun it round so my drawing was facing the wall. Now I like it. It is a symbol of how my brain works differently to most people's. At least, it's original. When I go home, I pay homage to witchy Kaiya with her own name pouring out of her head like Athena bursting out of Zeus' skull.

While I was getting taught about space and Henry VIII in school, I really got my proper education from my parents at home. In fact, my dad and I had a rule. If I could answer all his questions correctly, I could leave school forever. Obviously, this was a great ploy because he only posited questions that I would never learn the answers to in the confines of a classroom. Who invented reggae? How do computers work? Who was the first man on the moon? (That last one is a trick question; he considers Tintin's moon landing in the 1953 book takes precedence over the 1969 copycat mission.) I quickly realised that I would need to do a lot of work outside of school because there was so much I wasn't learning there. If only I had been born ten years later. Wikipedia could have broken me out of my educational bondage.

It was with my family that I learnt the power of storytelling. As poor people, the Stones had a lot of shit cars. You won't believe the number of childhood hours I spent in lay-bys. The Ford Focus will forever be a symbol of luxury travel. But before we got the Focus, we had a white Golf and the radio didn't work. Growing up, we lived pretty far away from my many, many relatives. Nana and Beardie lived four hours away near Bath and Jayne and the Boys were all the way in the thatched-cottaged Cotswolds. So we would regularly have to make a three-plus-hour drive to visit them.

In our filthy silent car, Cas and I would demand stories from my dad. The ones from his childhood were best. When he was naughty, or his parents were evil, or about music and computers from another time. But the best was the story about his granddad (Beardie's father). I'd met him once, in an old people's home. He was wrinkly and I was clearly an unobservant infant because that's all I remember.

Now, there is really only one story about my great-granddad. It is set in the late 1970s, my dad is nine and on holiday with his family, grandparents included. My great-granddad was a proud old poshie. He'd got a medal from the Queen, which proves it. They were staying in a hotel which may have been in Crete but more likely was some shit beach town in England that was 'quite sufficient'. The hotel had a pool on the roof, which to me hearing this story sounded like the height of sophistication – to be honest it still does.

The story goes that my great-granddad, Gordon, went up to the pool where my dad was already playing and, as he got out of the lift, my dad saw that the old man's gonad had popped out of his Speedos. That logically meant he'd been hanging out, shall we say, for the whole journey from his room to the rooftop, via a shared lift. My dad describes nearly pissing himself and being shushed by his parents and no one saying anything! Everyone politely averting their eyes from the singular wrinkly ball that had escaped like a smuggled sprout from a child's plate.

What happened? When did he realise?

The story is that apparently he didn't. He jumped into the pool, had a swim and when he got back out the offending knacker had been popped back into the old man's Speedos.

Now, I can't tell you how many times I've heard that story. It was a childhood myth, the stuff of real legend. I'm sure it's partly because it involved laughing at various words for testicles – balls, knackers, bollocks, gonads, etc. Maybe it was that this had happened to a rather un-humorous old man.

Oh and Gordon is a funny name because in the 1970s there was a comedy hit single called 'Gordon is a Moron'. My dad, aged eight, was singing the main refrain GORDON IS A MOOOORON – dancing around in his flares and wide-collared t-shirt, only to find his stern and rather angry grandfather standing behind him. Let's just say, Gordon dropped a bollock on more than one occasion.

Either way, the important thing is that there are stories that transcend human time and suffering, that bring serious and titled men to their knees (or at least can bring their serious and titled balls to their knees) and you can tell them without writing them down. Storytelling was a currency I was brought up with, and not just for car journeys. We tell each other about our days like we're recounting historic battles and we reminisce about things that happened long ago. I knew my father was a writer long before he ever published his first book because I had heard him for my whole life either telling us his own adventures or making up characters that did outrageous things.

Telling stories is a very human way of softening the blows of living: it made long car journeys fun for me and Cas; for my parents, I think it took the edge off driving to see old moody gits who disapproved of their life choices.

I will no doubt tell that story of my great-granddad to my children, maybe they will pass it down further – and essentially that's how all myths were invented. That's why Homer was not one man but many, many storytellers, and why writing isn't about spelling and grammar and pen licences.

CHAPTER 4

FALLING

By the end of primary school, I had learnt one thing for certain: I did not want to sit an entrance exam. For some reason, I was diametrically opposed to doing the eleven-plus. Everyone else in my class had tutors and were anxiously talking about catchment areas. They had been planning for years like doomsday preppers as if the practice papers and workbooks would save them. I just didn't get it and, more than that, it made me feel sick with nerves. Chrissy had moved in with her granny, not because her parents had nowhere to live, but so her address would be different. Aamna's mum told my mum *it was a pity we lived on the wrong side of the road.* If we were in the houses opposite we'd be in the right postcode for (said in hushed tones) *Heckmondwike Grammar.*

There were not many options for secondary schools since we had moved to Batley in 2004. Before the move

I was just going to the nearest mixed comp. But now most of the options that were available had ruled themselves out by being single sex. My parents were *never* going to send me to a girls' school. My mum had barely got through her time in one. She had been singled out as the troubled child who needed to be sent to a single-sex institution. It seems archaic to still be separating our children into arbitrary groups of boys and girls. A key part of my education had to be mingling with all types of people. Then the other option was religious schools. Again, my parents were not keen. Indoctrination and Catholic guilt were not high on their list for me. But here I was, refusing to take the exam for the best selective free grammar in the area. Which left one option: Batley Grammar.

Batley Grammar came highly recommended by a group of my parents' stoner friends: a handful of guys a bit younger than them who used to come round and play cards for hours at our kitchen table. These men knew each other from school. They had gone to Batley Grammar when it was also a selective free grammar in

the 1980s era. It had been a boys' school with excellent results. But at some point, it started to accept girls and had become fee-paying. Qam, Matt and Brad told my parents about how their school days had been the best of their lives. My parents were beguiled; they'd never heard anyone talk about their school years like that before. And it was five minutes from our house. All they wanted was that we went to somewhere we enjoyed and gave us a good education. They wanted our learning experience to be different from theirs.

But there was a problem. There was absolutely no way my parents could afford to send me to a private school. We had only just about managed to move out into our own house. Some jobs had proven momentarily profitable for my dad. He had been sent to North Korea to direct some children's animation. But, unsurprisingly, the man who was always late paying wages, and when he did it was in thick wads of cash in envelopes under Chinese restaurant tables, turned out to be an unreliable (and dodgy) employer. Mr Kim had disappeared and, once again, we were poor. But for me this was normal. Long spells of my parents arguing and refusing to get real jobs. Looking back now, as an adult, it appears we lived on an edge, sometimes having enough money for things and sometimes, more frequently, not. I was never in want of anything. But if you don't ask for things, you aren't going to be disappointed. Plus, I knew that if I really wanted or needed something, ends would meet. My parents' own childhood wants still loomed large in their minds. The knock-off Action Man without moveable hands, the wrong dungarees. Poverty is not just the want of something but the getting of the wrong thing, the ersatz, the version off the market.

Then came the *sign*. Gordon's wife, my great-grandmother died. Primrose was an eccentric, a *goer*, in my dad's words. She left him a lump of money, certainly the most money he'd ever had before. Maybe it was because she felt guilty for the time she had made him eat a pig's trotter and he'd had to bite round its massive toenail. Adoo took that money and basically decided to invest it. Not in stocks and shares because we don't know how to do that sort of thing. No, he put it aside to pay for school for me and Cas (until I later became a scholarship kid). That money covered things like school trips, new shoes, uniforms and the fees. But this money meant that I didn't have to take the eleven-plus. I could go to a non-religious mixed school without having to sit an exam.

Now, I must have known that I would have failed the eleven-plus. Even then I understood that I was clever but that I had trouble proving it. I hated those comprehension tests. Point, evidence, explanation – bullshit. Now I know that the kids who got in had months of training with tutors who taught them the tricks. I don't believe in private education – I definitely benefited from mine, but I think it's morally dubious. It is an unfair advantage in life. However, I'd also like to respectfully point out that people find all sorts of ways of paying to make sure their kids get the best. The best state schools are in areas where you pay via postcode. The selective free schools are fed by families who pay ridiculous amounts for long-term tutors (an industry which I profit from… more about that later). I don't have the answers, unless I'm five pints deep. But I do think that one arbitrary exam at the age of ten shouldn't decide if you go to the 'clever' school or not.

Batley is what I only half-affectionately call *the arse-end of Yorkshire*. It's not York or Harrogate, where your great-aunt retired to, surrounded by Betty's Tea Rooms and stretches of countryside. In fact, it's near Bradford so it's much more ethnically diverse than some other towns in Yorkshire.

Batley is grey. Not because of concrete – in fact, the historic sandstone buildings, mills and factories are golden and beautiful. But because they have stood empty for at least the decade I lived there. It is grey with absence of care. It is a neglected place. The train station sits at the end of a cobbled street which makes cars shake, so people would rather just drive the extra five minutes to the next station or get a bus. Or if they had any sense at all they would avoid the place entirely.

In Year 7, we did a walking tour of the town for geography. It felt fancy (a school trip in the first week!). It was exactly the sort of exciting perk one might expect from a *fee-paying school*. But the trip consisted of just one activity: stopping at desolate places. *This used to be a tram station. This used to be a shoddy mill. This used to be a mine. Look at the way the houses here are stained from the factory fumes.* They closed it down in 1973 but we're still filthy from it. We were essentially told we were living in a place that once had an identity.

There is no doubt that there is still a great deal of personality in Batley. But growing up, it felt like the land time forgot. Not that it froze, stuck in one era, but rather that it aged and decayed and nobody gave a fuck. As you drive into the town there is a big arch with two bats sat carved into the top. But their wings have been lopped off. I spent a lot of time feeling like those bats would have fucked off to be mascots of some other town if they could have.

If the tour was in any way comprehensive, here's what else we would have seen: the Wetherspoon's on the corner, always busy with old men waiting for opening in the morning. After the smoking ban they stood outside, furious that their routines had been changed for something as poncey as the benefit of other people's lungs. Mr Scrivens ought to have shown us the new and shiny 24-hour Tesco Extra with two floors and bridge to the high street. It destroyed its rival supermarket branch, a Netto, not more than 200 metres away. He should have pointed out the high street where each shop slowly bit the dust over the decade I lived there. The town's Wikipedia page even marks the date the Woolworths, where I bought Wayne Wonder's hit single 'No Letting Go', closed down. We didn't watch the souped-up drug dealer cars zooming up and down the main roads.

And lastly, you can't talk about Batley without a nod to the Fox's biscuit factory. Only sometimes, never frequently enough, it would pump out the smell of sweet dough and melted chocolate. But inside there was nothing resembling the fantastical Willy Wonka. It was just ladies in hair nets putting Jam 'n' Creams and Viennesses into the plastic trays for the Christmas selection boxes.

It is difficult to try to explain my time in Batley. That I loved it and hated it with all the same parts of myself. I am anxious about having to try to sum up one of the most complex parts of who I am. I am inordinately proud of where I grew up. I would not be who I am if I had not spent my formative years there. But on the other hand, it was grim. I was incredibly unhappy living in Batley and I was preoccupied with leaving as soon as I could. I don't have to imagine growing up there. I did it, however distant I have tried to make it feel.

In secondary school, my identity was solidified for me. I was a know-it-all, even though I wasn't good enough to back up the label. After being called *nerd* and *book-buster*, I had no choice but to take on the mantle of being clever. But that just made it more complicated when I failed to actually live up to that epithet. There were much more consistent high performers in my classes. But they were quiet. My problem was enthusiasm.

I always had ideas, suggestions and an arm up.

Then my personal brand expanded to weirdness. A girl from a primary school I'd thought I had left long behind ended up in the same class as me. I was happy to see her until she brought up the layers thing again. I think that's why I am firmly attached to my statement bob these days. No fucking layers. Later, when I chopped my hair off, I was weird for having short hair. I was weird because I didn't like the right music. I was weird because I made jokes and I would be the only person laughing.

I had a terrifically bad puberty. Being a teenager was a plague. From my perspective of narrator of this story, it feels like it must have transformed me. I don't think I was an angry child. My parents talk of me as this sweet thing but high school and hormones and other teenagers forced me to build some protective bark around my softness. A better writer than I would call it a carapace.

My new body was tricky to sit in. I had never particularly mastered the old one either. I was the child in school with a hole in the knees of brand-new trousers and tights a week into September. I had scabby knees. For Christmas one year I asked my Granny Jayne for

a 'bum pad' – like knee pads but a big pillow you strap to your bum for when you fall backwards (of course). Unfortunately, it didn't exist, but I feel there was a gap in the market. I had roller blades and decided that if you fell backwards rather than forwards you could save your face, knees and hands by just sacrificing your arse. It only took one downhill tumble to understand why people didn't do that. My fall was cartoon-like: my legs bicycling, making invisible circles in the air, before thumping down on my derrière. You hit your coccyx which is where all the nerves at the bottom of your spine nestle safely. When you topple back, you can't stop the back of your head from pounding into the pavement. I learnt my lesson the hard way. But the thing about being an accident-prone child is that everyone just says you'll grow out of it.

When I hit puberty if anything it got worse. I finally managed to graduate to my first broken bone – ice-skating, of course. After a decade of hospital trips, where a nurse would scathingly look at my swollen ankles and twisted wrists, my parents assured me that I hadn't actually broken a bone. Forty-eight hours later, I started getting pins and needles undulating up my arm, and my dad took me to A&E. I left smug and in a cast. At school, I won a hat-trick of black eyes. I kicked my standing foot rather than the ball in a competitive game of breaktime footy. I toppled like a bicycle and had to walk around with a newly thick brow mottled with an impressive green bruise. But worst of all was the smashed teeth. Bolting round the corner of the sports hall with the enthusiasm of a Year 7, my new Kickers slipped. My face took the brunt of the fall – more specifically, my front teeth. One snapped clean in half and the rest seemed to move. I had to have braces and a temporary tooth made of filling.

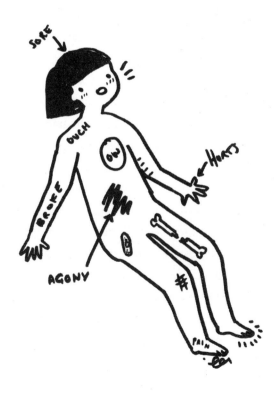

There was a pretty convincing theory put forward by my mum for all these injuries. I had a new body. I had always been tall but I shot up further and quicker, leaving everyone behind. But my period seemed to take forever to show. Just as I was starting to feel left behind it arrived. Suddenly out bedoing'ed my tits. Not just some cute little lumps, but in two months I went from a B cup to a DD (think teaspoons of jam to those wobbling ornate Victorian jellies). It didn't help that at 5 ft 9 (OK, 5 ft 8 and a half) my size 5 feet didn't lend me much of a solid base. So I was led to believe that it was really just a waiting game until I was used to this vessel that would see me through until I got old and familiar with my body again.

But, of course, that is bullshit. I have had to learn to love the fall. I embrace the floor and the adrenaline. I have learnt never to look back at what tripped you up because very rarely is there an answer and even more rarely does it make you feel any better. I have accepted that sometimes people rush to help and others walk past snickering – both are humiliating and kind. And in some horrible, questionable way, the ache and the sting of cuts and bruises makes me feel a little more alive and a little more present in my body. But other things sit painfully. Knocked-over drinks, smashed plates, split rice bags, slopped food, dropped glasses, all still fill me with dread. They are illuminated arrows pointing at my inability to control my limbs.

In my mid-teens, I began to fixate on old cinema. Black-and-white was good but even better were silent films. I liked how words had been removed, that a universal language of melodrama replaced verbose explanations. The pinnacle of all this was Charlie Chaplin. I loved the slapstick. It's freeing to watch someone with even less luck than you. Each smack, blow and thud reminded me I was not alone. I still think if all these creative endeavours fail and I have to get a real adult job, I can always re-train to be a clown.

Teenage girls are both evil and genius. I love teenagers. It's not a widely held opinion. They have a potency and an affinity for the extreme which I have never really grown out of. Melodrama is a currency we share. It manifests in my adult self as hot-headed judgement, brashness and revelling in sweeping unsubstantiated generalisations.

Adolescence is also the ultimate vulnerability. We are left wondering who our friends are, how to grasp the terrifying thought of independence and tackling how we are seen by the outside world. It can leave you in a permanent out-of-body experience, constantly weighing yourself to someone else's standards. I think that the inherent core-shaking experience of being a teenager can make people vindictive. The opportunity to be mean, to take a dig at someone else, acts as a momentary cure for their own sense of inadequacy and their own pain.

But – oh boy – it is hard to be on the receiving end of that. Even if you can tell yourself that it is not about you, it is hard to get through each day when you are the scapegoat for a room full of anguish.

Because I fell over a lot, I used to think that in many ways it would be easier to be physically attacked. I was used to bruises and bleeding. But the emotional torment was something I felt that I was not equipped to deal with.

In many ways, I don't want to write about the specifics of what was said and done to me. Partly because of the deep fear that, if I am explicit, I'll be told once again that I was overreacting and that maybe I deserved it. Partly because I don't want to give the torment any more of my time. And maybe in the deepest corners of myself I feel like I'm giving the world ammunition. But it is important to give the details.

It started with someone else being bullied. She was my friend and she lived on a pig farm, and that alone gave people enough material to rip her apart. The group of girls who were picking on her were 'nice' girls. By that I mean they did well in school, they didn't get in trouble, they were pretty and largely middle class. They came from ostensibly functioning homes. But they modelled themselves proudly on the Plastics from *Mean Girls*. They hadn't picked up on the satire.

One particular morning, my friend was on the end of some particularly slicing remarks and I lost my temper. I said *no*. I refused to believe this was how we treated one another. They looked at me with shock. I left the room feeling like I had won, that I had stood up for my friend. But the real consequence was that the focus turned on me and my friend turned too, no doubt joining in because she was relieved to no longer be the target. The jokes about pig shit quickly dwindled and a laser vision was focused on my every move. I walked funny, I mispronounced words, I was too clever, my face was too round, I looked like a man, I was a man, I was a dyke. My name was weird so people would mispronounce it. But it got worse. I tried to keep it in and not to react. But what I could not control was the shame. All those eyes on me and I could do nothing except for igniting bright red.

When she blushes all you have to do is count down from ten and she'll be crying by one.

...and that is how fun new games are invented. Not one person said a thing. When it happened once in class and once in a school play rehearsal, the adult witnesses said *nothing*.

At the height of my agony, after nights awake dreading the next day, I went to my form tutor. I told him how unhappy I was, that the girls in my class were causing me so much pain with their asides, their pointed remarks about me. He told me to try to fit in more. That if I didn't give them a reaction they would get bored... The gaps in that advice rang louder than the words. He didn't need to say that with their boredom would come another victim. He didn't need to say that I was weird so brought it upon myself. He didn't need to say that he didn't really believe that it was that bad. Because it was loud and clear.

I went to the deputy headmistress and she offered me much of the same, but raised the advice to new heights. *If you stopped crying, then they would leave you alone.* The blame was firmly placed on me. She made it clear that she thought that I was a crybaby and an over-sensitive, over-reacting one at that. I still am a crybaby and proud of it. Why did I have to change who I was to stop this? Why was I being punished twice? Once by thirteen-year-olds, who were replicating the words and shaming that we can only presume they were enduring themselves out of sight, and then once again by the adults in charge. I left the room wishing that I had been punched because then at least I'd have evidence.

Why do I feel so much? I cried to my mum that night. She sat and pondered, stroking my hair.

It is a gift to feel this much, she told me. But lying there it felt like a heavy burden to try to contain all that was boiling within me. I couldn't imagine a time when I might be able to safely restrain the overflow and, today, I still can't. I can hold the feelings better but repression isn't my strong suit.

All the while, my class was heralded as the *nicest in the school*. I realised that no one was going to save me. Lying awake at night, I was a monument of dread frozen by the prospect of the next day, and the one after that. We looked for new schools but the options were too thin and too far away. When I came home each afternoon my parents were on the receiving end of my rage. I screamed and sobbed and burnt. They didn't know how to help, they'd gone into the school and spoken to the teachers. Nothing changed.

It will never be like this again. It will never be as bad as this ever again. You can get through this.

At the end of the school year, I was done. A gleeful countdown began again and like Pavlov's Dog I started to weep on cue. Though, today was different. I turned not away from them but towards them. I climbed onto a table and I began to scream…

You are so unhappy with yourselves that you have to pick on me. Well, just because I'm the victim now doesn't mean that you're safe. You all hate each other with a passion and will betray your so-called friends just so that it doesn't happen to you. Well, it will.

I'm not sure I managed to be quite as cohesive or articulate as that, plus with hindsight I wonder how much could be understood between my snotty sobs. But I know that they understood when I pointed and concluded: *Each and every one of you is a cunt who will die alone.*

They pretty much let me be after that. I don't think because my words had some transformative effect, showering them with self-awareness and compassion. But it probably triggered the realisation that perhaps I was unhinged. Fear is a great equaliser. If only a teacher had told me all I needed to do was stand on a table and throw around some expletives, I might have got some sleep that year. I have never been prouder of myself. In moments of chaos, fear and sadness, I think about thirteen-year-old Kaiya and that she saved herself in the only way she knew how.

I'd like to talk about the teachers who seemed to think it was in their job description to try to destroy my hopes and dreams. I had lost a lot of faith in adults as well as in my peers. I had seen teachers repeatedly ignore homophobic slurs in class. I'd even been told that I shouldn't be upset about comments because after all it wasn't true, right? But beyond just a failure to care for the emotional wellbeing of their students, some of the teachers (I'll talk about the good ones soon, I promise) also seemed to think that their duty was to teach children to obey and regurgitate. Education, in their eyes, was about teaching kids a lesson.

When I started secondary school, I had been desperate to study English properly – with teachers who

taught specific subjects. I wanted to read books and talk about them with adults who had chosen to devote their life to exploring stories. I was excited for creative writing and to read Shakespeare and poems. It all sounded very adult. I viewed it as the start of my career as a writer and presumably it would be something I'd be good at it. I'd been reading for years. God, I couldn't wait.

When I actually started, I came across the greatest enemy to adult literacy and the enjoyment of reading and writing – English teachers.

My first was Mr Fisher, the form tutor who failed to help me even slightly when I was bullied. Before that I didn't really mind him. He was mainly embarrassing in that way that only old white men manage to be. For example, he would describe passages of a book as *sexy*, in my eyes a crime punishable by death. Worse than this, Mr Fisher seemed to believe that knowledge was something one owned or held like a physical object. It sat in his hand and we, his lowly wards, had nothing at all to offer. It was this understanding of knowledge which meant that he was able to frequently tell me (and others, no doubt) that we were wrong. Slowly, my indifference turned into rage.

We had a heated discussion when I questioned why the school had more assemblies a week split by religion than we did as a united student body. The two options on Mondays and Fridays were the Christian assembly or the Muslim assembly – an odd arbitrary divide which left the non-believers, Sikh and Hindu kids to decide where to go… (clue: white kids in one room, PoC in another). My main issue was that I hated the Christian assemblies. Mr Fisher later retaliated by writing a 'think piece' for the school newsletter about tradition and the need to keep alive old institutions such as hymns and the Bible. I thought it was a pretty lame move.

It bled into lessons. For coursework, we were asked to design a stage for J.B. Priestley's *An Inspector Calls*. He prescriptively told us exactly what to do. I tried to be inventive and made up a third-wall-breaking concept (not that I knew what one of those was) where the audience were placed behind a two-way mirror to watch the scene unravel; he marked me down for being anachronistic. At parents' evening, Mr Fisher made me cry when he told my mum I was lazy, that I didn't read things properly, that I was clever but didn't bother following it through. I began to hate English.

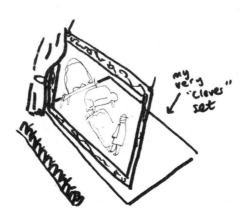

my very "clever" set

He retired early. I hoped that this meant that I could get back into what I thought should be my favourite subject. He was being replaced, like lots of the old men in the school, by a new graduate, someone who seemed to want to be there and who actually liked children.

But that bubble burst quickly too. Miss Radcliffe hated me. I'm not sure why. Maybe because I had hung round after class early into term and asked her about which novels we were studying. I had just read *The Catcher in the Rye* and loved it because I too was an adolescent full of rage who thought I was surrounded by phoneys. But she said she wasn't a fan of it. Fair – it is a bit pompous. What about *1984*? She hadn't read it and I was too unworldly to hide my surprise.

I thought I was clever too, so maybe it was that. Know-it-alls are insufferable and the turn of events that followed after my GCSEs ensured that I dropped that particular persona pretty quick. But this teacher also took it as her responsibility to knock me down a peg or two. So she would ask the class if anyone else had an answer when I was the only one with my hand up. *Anyone else? Someone other than Kaiya?* Miss Radcliffe preferred to move on, leaving me hanging rather than let me speak.

Teachers have a sacred responsibility: to uplift. But for many of us, we are not that lucky. We have to face teachers who gaslight us. We have been repeatedly told that we are one thing: lazy, thick as shit, stupid, slow, a waste of space. It comes from the mouths of people we trust, friends, family and teachers. It takes so much to not be pushed into apathy or pushed into fulfilling those labels. The energy required to resist is enormous. Often it takes years before we realise we have been lied to. And that is if we're lucky enough to twig later on. Too many adults go through life with the weight of being told who they were by teachers; it is a heavy burden. But, please remember, it is lies. You are not stupid. You are not lazy. You are not a lost cause. We have been caught and tangled in the net of teachers' ignorance and laziness. We have tied our self-worth to their statements and at some point we must begin the slow and arduous process of breaking free and seeing that we are more than they said we were.

At school, I was wise enough to keep my ambitions of writing close to my chest, nestled away in a deep corner of myself. It was a secret I knew, if let out into the world, would be crushed. It felt so delicate that even one joke or comment could have suffocated the tiny flames. It didn't come up mainly because we didn't do much creative writing in English lessons; I can think of only a handful of incidents. The last was ahead of our GCSEs.

Write about a journey.

The year of my GCSEs I was fifteen. I came out of school and, as always, my dad was in the car waiting to pick me and Cas up. As we drove down Carlinghow

Hill towards home he said *I think I found my birth father today.*

It had been ten years since he had found Jayne, and I knew he had spent time trying to find his dad, but the name Michael Taylor was an impossible obstacle. But that day, Adoo typed in Michael Stuart Brough Taylor (the name on his birth certificate under Father) into Facebook and someone had popped up. That evening, we all crowded round the computer looking at a website linked to the account. There was a photo of a man with my dad's eyes and even more weirdly – the same facial hair.

The Stones always spent a long time contemplating and theorising about who we were. It was already a teenage pastime. But it felt so rare and magical to have an answer, rather than just another question. So when we were asked to write about a journey in class, I knew I had to write about the four-and-a-half-hour road trip that dad and I took. In one day, we drove from Batley to Bognor Regis and back to meet my great-grandmother (his grandmother) for the first time. My essay was soppy and sloppy. Full of sentimentality that is unavoidable when you're fifteen. But I also described how on the way down we laughed and made jokes nervously, awaiting a revelation. I wrote about one of those moments after which nothing can ever be the same. It was the first very personal thing I ever wrote and showed anyone. When I handed it in, Miss

Radcliffe returned it with a note: *I don't understand why you would describe your grandmother as an alien. Your grammar needs work.*

Luckily, my skin had grown thick with years of comments about my spelling and grammar. I had an adolescent self-assuredness that I was simply misunderstood and in the wrong place. I left feeling like I had written something I could be proud of because she hated it, so I must be doing something right. When she praised someone else's work about their first shiny red bike, I knew I just had the wrong crowd here. I am so thankful that I had louder voices telling me that I wasn't bad or stupid. Otherwise, I think I might have been at risk of never writing another word after that.

CHAPTER 5

FAILING

Something odd happened in my first parents' evening at Batley Grammar. For some reason, the school asked the Year 7s not to attend, so my parents went off in their jeans and trainers to meet all my teachers. It must be a horrible time warp to leave school in a fury, swearing blind that you'll never set foot in an institution like that again, only to find yourself returning via your spawn. In that first parents' evening, my physics teacher told my parents that I was special and that I was *Oxbridge material*. This man had never indicated to me that he thought I was anything out of the ordinary, which is probably for the best – it would have gone to my head. I was already at risk of being insufferable. I was surfing the mixed messages being sent my way, which resulted in the constant oscillation of extreme self-confidence and painful self-doubt. I clung to any tiny piece of affirmation and metaphorically pinned it above my bed – much like your recently divorced aunt does on Facebook.

I have always imagined that this was a throwaway comment that got out of hand.

But my parents returned home and repeated that phrase *Oxbridge material* to me. It meant no more to me aged eleven than it did to my parents. We had to work out that it wasn't one place but two very old universities that seemed to have some sort of mystic power thus deserving its own term. This lack of knowledge was not some momentary lapse but a chasm. It was just the edge and the glimpse into a different world. My mum googled it and took it to mean I should be aiming for the best, a thought already in their heads but without the vocabulary of academic success. Mr Miller sat with us and set me on a particular track. I was impressed and my parents were impressed, because neither of them had a degree, or even A-levels, at that point. So for every snide comment from one teacher, there was the constant internal rebuttal. Someone had said I was going to be a writer, another teacher said I was Oxbridge material, and my parents say I'm bound for greatness (thanks for the achievable goals). I chose to believe the good stuff. How else was I supposed to survive?

Now, the fun bit, I get to write about the teachers who waved my flag, wore my colours and made up chants on the sideline of my symbolic sports match.

The greatest thing about my school was that we had a classics department. By that I mean a bulwark of a woman who single-handedly kept this very niche subject alive. Classics is the study of ancient civilisations, their history, art and literature. In the past, my school also taught Latin and Greek but it had fallen out of fashion. The head of classics kept the subject afloat by teaching the subject in English (classical civilisations) and by consistently getting the best GCSE and A-level grades of any subject in the school. It was by far the most popular humanities subject for A-level.

Mrs Wilson was a petite woman coming up to retirement. If I were to guess, she was almost certainly an Autumn, in Colour Me Beautiful terms. No one could rock a burnt umber silk scarf better than her.

Despite her slight frame, everyone, pupils and teachers alike, were terrified of her.

There is something special about a strict authority figure, and I say this as someone who is not a big fan of power hierarchies. It just seemed to me that the teachers who were the harshest were in most ways the fairest. They had sometimes ridiculous arbitrary rules but they were honest about the consequences – if you do X, Y will happen. But you have to give very clear instructions to enforce such a world, and I think that suits me. I have also always found that the strictest teachers are the most compassionate and generous with extra help. Plus, with my two favourite teachers (Mrs Wilson and Mr Hussain), their strictness was always about getting the most out of us. Funnily enough, the scariest, strictest teachers in my experience never shamed me. They lifted me up.

Classics was a revelation for me. I had never been the sort of child who was really into myths, partly because I had never been taught them in primary school. But what is not to love about stories about gods that behave badly, mythical creatures and heroes. As we moved through the years, the topics expanded. We looked at the history and started reading original literature (in translation) and I realised that it had all of the things I loved. It was an expansive subject and my enthusiasm was only encouraged. When we read photocopied sections of Ovid's *Amores* – which is a bit like an ancient love advice column – Mrs Wilson lent me her copy of the whole book. She handed it to me saying to watch out for the saucy bits. Aged fourteen, all I wanted was ancient writings with double entendres and adults winking at the bits of the world that I was starting to step into.

Plus, Mrs Wilson's lessons were fun. They always involved drawing and re-telling stories or looking at ancient artefacts. In some ways, as I got older I wondered if it was too easy or too childish. Especially when teachers had begun to talk darkly about GCSEs and university and academic achievement. In other subjects, things were desolately serious and all about answers and techniques. But in Mrs Wilson's classroom, the coloured pencils were always out. With hindsight that's perhaps why I loved it. It was freeing and it appealed to my love of education rather than the oppressive system of grade-marking, levels and grammar that dominated lots of my other lessons. More than just that, Mrs Wilson took it deadly seriously. Here was this woman who could silence a room full of fighting sixteen-year-olds with one look and she was getting excited about the sort of magical herb Hermes gave Odysseus to prevent Circe turning him into a pig (it's moly, if you're interested or inordinately worried about turning into a pig).

That passion is contagious. When I decided in Year 9 that classics was going to be my thing, other teachers sort of suggested it was a waste. A PE teacher pointed out with my grades I could be a pharmacist, the height of the school's ambitions. But I didn't want to think about getting a job or careers. I had absolutely no ambition to do anything remotely sensible like law or medicine. I just wanted to leave Batley as quick as I could and by any means necessary.

There was a funny club that one French teacher set up called Culture Vultures. We went to musicals, ballets and occasionally obscure opera for cheap because of school group tickets. My parents knew they could never afford to take me and Cas to these sorts of things as a family but they made sure I could go with Mr Wilby's group. I never missed a show and so when the original National Tour of *The History Boys* made its way to Sheffield, he let me go despite its *adult content*. It was one of the few times in my life that I saw something of myself reflected on the stage. It felt like I'd been hit by a bag of pianos when Posner said: *I'm Jewish, I'm small, I'm a homosexual and I'm from Sheffield. I'm fucked.* It's only two out of five for me, but it felt closer than anything else I had encountered before. It was all I could think about for the coming weeks. I felt a kinship with Alan Bennett and being an outsider in my little corner of Yorkshire. I'd not ever thought about the possibility of being queer because it wasn't an option. So much of it was subconscious recognition but it rang a bell loud within me. It connected that throwaway comment from the physics teacher to this world of thinking differently and arguing and education as something other than marks out of ten.

I think it is important to note that I did, albeit briefly, do all the usual British teenage things. I had dabbled in being an emo – the subcultural chic of the early noughties. But I didn't want to dye my hair black nor did I have the money for the required minimum three studded belts. This period of time coincided with my trips to Leeds on a Saturday. We would hang out with the other usually much older teenagers who also wore all black. We'd spend hours chatting on MSN and redesigning our Myspace pages, only to meet in person and stand in awkward silence and then head to Greggs for a sausage, cheese and bean pasty. There weren't many of us who did this from my school and so I was able to build a sense of self beyond my classroom experiences. I used to buy the younger-looking teens fags (when you could smoke at sixteen) and aged thirteen I got served for the first time in a Lidl. We sat in a triangle of grass between the motorway and a retail park on the outskirts of the city and five of us shared the two-litre bottle of lukewarm scrumpy. Other days we would endlessly walk around the shops or talk of parties. If it rained, we would walk round the Royal Armouries until we found the Armoured Elephant glistening under the weight of thousands of panels. I always pondered how this creature had ended up here in Leeds with its sad golden eyes like a trunked grim reaper and the faceless riders on his back.

But as I got older things changed. The Corn Exchange was gutted. The owners kicked out all the shops selling sex toys and incense and tried to start a food court. The community of vampiric teens were moved on. I moved on.

The introduction of wireless internet had already transformed the world as we knew it. When we replaced our babbling modem, it brought about a profound change for my household. It meant the free and easy access to information. My dad continued to put his work up online (always an early adopter) and an online zine he made got some real traction. He got a literary agent and eventually his first book deal. But it was Wilma Stone who really took it by the horns. She decided to do a degree at the local art school. She worked very hard to get in and continued grafting through the course. A fellow student's younger brother had got into Oxford. My mum relayed the information that he used to wake up every day at 6 a.m. before school to revise for his A-levels. We took this information as gospel and so, as I entered into Year 11, I began getting up before even the sun had crawled up.

My parents took it in turns to wake up with me and make me a coffee as I would work the extra hour before heading to school. When I came home, I had tea with my family and then returned to my desk. It felt normal. My dad worked at home and his desk was along from mine. My mum was learning new skills, filling sketchbooks and reading critical theory for the first time. So all three of us just worked together. It was the living encapsulation of what I had been told growing up – *the most important things in life are Family and Work.* At weekends, we would watch films in the evenings but there was a lot of productivity in the Stone household.

I never once breathed a word about my early morning work sessions to anyone at school. I was predicted A*s across the board for my GCSEs. I didn't find the work particularly hard but there was so much of it and it took me a long time to absorb the information. When

I went to sit my exams, I went in knowing I was going to do well. On results day, I was satisfied. It sounds odd but I was quietly disappointed that I had dropped a couple of the stars off the As of history and English. Two subjects I had thought were my best.

I had been debating where to go for my A-levels. I was not particularly happy at my small school. There was an excellent sixth form college with 2,000 students around the corner. But it didn't teach classics. I knew that I could apply for classics without the A-level in the subject because most schools don't teach it. But I couldn't imagine spending two years not studying with Mrs Wilson. So I stayed on.

The summer before starting my A-levels, I went to Latin Camp. It was one of the million things my mum had found on the Internet about improving my chances of getting into Oxford. She had quite rightly pointed out that if I went to Oxford to study classics most of the kids would be from posh schools and would have studied at least one of the ancient languages. The Oxford University website assured us that it wouldn't be an unfair advantage but we thought I'd better find out if I even liked it before I sunk all this time into it. Luckily, there was a wonderful group called the Joint Association of Classics Teachers (JACT) and they ran summer schools for kids who are beginners to Latin and Ancient Greek. Not just that, but they had great scholarships.

When I arrived at Wells Cathedral School, I began to realise that most of the world really was not like Batley. I had suspected it for quite a while but when I looked around the boarding school we were staying in, I really understood that I wasn't in Kansas any more. I met a lot of posh people for the first time and it was weird. It sort of felt like they were LARPing an Enid Blyton book. They all played the piano and sang in choirs at the little chapels attached to their schools. They had names like Tosca, Boris and Biddie. Lots of them were used to staying in the boarding houses we were put up in with four sets of bunk beds and neatly lined-up desks. More importantly, they had been doing Latin and Greek for at least five years. On the other hand, I did not even know what prep school was.

The first two hours felt horribly intimidating. But as soon as I was put in a beginners' class, it all changed. We were going to cover four school years of Latin teaching in ten days. I had a great young teacher who brought out all the good stuff about Latin – the sex, wild history and explicit poems. I was in a class with older people, they were all eighteen and about to head to Oxford to study classics. But, like me, they were not from posh schools. It was the first time I'd met people who were accessibly older than me. To me they seemed so clever and cool.

We did our classes and then sat together after working. I hadn't really ever got to do that before. Work was something I did alone. Jim would improvise songs about us all. Helen was warm and funny. Lorna had planned to do medicine but suddenly changed her mind. Scott had been a postman and was about to start at Oxford as a mature student. Lucy was the same age as me and was just as ambitious. But perhaps more importantly, they saw me differently than anyone else had before. It was at Wells that someone told me that I was funny for the first time in my life. I had never before been *funny*. My crude, rude comments and asides had been met with *evils* at school – *Why do you have to be such a freak all the time, Kaiya?* But here I could make people actually laugh. We sat in the sun and did Latin, eating ice cream, and it felt like the first summer I'd ever had since becoming a teenager.

Another important thing happened as I pushed out through my mid-teens and approached the ending of compulsory education. I started receiving the Education Maintenance Allowance (EMA). The EMA was a Labour government initiative to encourage students to stay in education past GCSEs. It was means-tested and gave the poorest students a weekly allowance dependent on their attendance in their educational institution. I received the largest possible amount of £30 a week. I had never really had a regular amount of money; there was one six-month period of time when I got pocket money but generally I had to ask my parents for a tenner here and there. That, and any birthday and Christmas money, were my teenage income.

But entering into sixth form all that changed. Thirty pounds a week was unimaginable wealth for me. I could buy clothes and makeup and go out for dinner with my mates. While previously I never really felt poor, I was aware of the differing financial worlds my friends and I lived in. My school was filled with kids with either working-class parents who had climbed the social ladder or middle-class aspirationals. Brands were king. Perhaps out of an internal understanding that if I wanted them I couldn't have the Uggs or the Juicy Couture or the Louis Vuitton handbag, I decided that I was completely uninterested in that world. If I didn't want much then I couldn't be disappointed.

For sixth form, my classes shrunk significantly. Even though my class groups were tiny, my teachers just assumed I was fine. They worried about the other kids. There was just an expectation that I worked hard and that would be enough. I thought exactly the same. Mrs Wilson, however, characteristically went the extra mile. She taught me, Daniel Murray and Samuel Paley (another keen kid) Latin GCSE in her spare time. She wanted us to be her last hurrah before retiring.

My other favourite teacher was Mr Hussain. At the time, he was the only Muslim teacher in the school, which was just one reason why he was notable. The second reason was that he was nearly as feared as Mrs Wilson. He stalked corridors and enforced uniform rules draconically. I was terrified of him for the two years he didn't teach me, but as with all ominous figures I was morbidly fascinated by him. Eventually, he became my history teacher and he remained so until I left school aged seventeen. What was shocking about him was that he was very relaxed in his classroom. He appeared to have the armour of a severe guard in the corridors but in his room he was different. In one of our early classes he tested us – asking what a child born out of wedlock was called. Never one to hold back from testing boundaries and swearing, I piped up. Perhaps everyone else didn't know, but when I exclaimed *Bastard* their eyes widened. Some particularly melodramatic girls, with GHD-straight

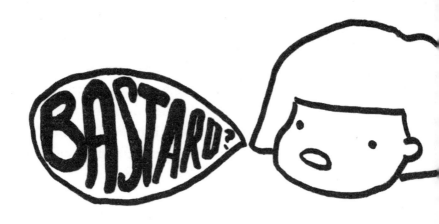

hair, gasped. They eagerly awaited my punishment but it never came. My answer was just met by a knowing smile. I knew from then that we would get on.

In his classroom, debate was king. I am not a fan of *devil's advocate* in real life. It is often used as a tool to question people's lived experience, to try to pretend that the world should be objective. Really objective just means that some old white guy has said something in such a way as to pretend that his opinion has not been informed by his own very limited life view. But I think I learnt more from having my arguments rigorously questioned by Mr Hussain than I ever did with all my other teachers put together. It wasn't about the facts or simply having information, it was about how you could use it and manipulate it. I guess one could call it critical thinking. One of his favourite things to do was to split the classroom and get us to argue the opposite of what we believed. His least favourite thing was marking, which he didn't do.

Once in class, Emma Elton asked who the smartest student Mr Hussain had ever taught was.

Daniel Murray.

What – not Kaiya? She looked at me wickedly. I would be lying if I said I wasn't absolutely gutted. It's not a competition, but I had lost.

Daniel Murray was in the year above me and in sixth form we became mates. In some ways, we were very similar. He too was obsessed with classics and wanted to study it at university. He was the other kid with a full scholarship but he had to share a bedroom with his two brothers. He used to joke that all of his adult clothes came from a bin bag that a man had given his dad in the pub. It wasn't a joke. He once showed me the pub. But Mr Hussain was right; Daniel was definitely more clever than me. I was so jealous of his memory and his ability to write things down. We bonded because we both had big aspirations that seemed to be above our stations.

Oxford and Cambridge were not on our school's horizons. Everyone seemed to go to either Leeds University or Leeds Metropolitan, depending on the grades. But Mrs Wilson drove us both in her own car on a Saturday to Oxford for an open day, and a couple of months later Daniel came with me and my parents to look round Cambridge. I settled on Oxford because I liked the course and it was near London. I wanted to be near a city; I worried about being suffocated by the smallness and the beauty of a town. Daniel picked Cambridge and a college where our deputy headmaster had assured us that they would like us as the college had links to Yorkshire.

This really is the evidence that my school had no idea about Oxbridge. But for Daniel and a few other kids in his year, the senior staff decided that they would try for the first time in decades to get some pupils into Cambridge. When the interviews were offered to a couple of applicants, the headmistress congratulated them in assembly. Off Daniel went to Cambridge. He came back disheartened. He didn't get in. The chips on our shoulders grew heavier. The following months were awful. He was so depressed. *I never had a chance, they don't want people like us.* I was gutted – if anyone deserved it I was sure it was Daniel. I still think that.

But the blow didn't just affect him; the school took it as a sign. Oxbridge didn't want anything to do with us. I was told not to apply. My form tutor explicitly said: *If Daniel didn't manage it, why would they want you? It's a waste of an option.*

I feel like there was this very odd attitude that ambition was something to be ashamed of. It feels sewn into the local identity. We tell ourselves that we live in *God's Own Country*, that we're friendlier, better, less poncey than down south. But with that comes the acceptance of not just being the underdog but being the righteous dejected, the martyred denied, the no-winners. Our holiness comes from our lack of ambition. God forbid you show a twinkling of wanting something more: *who do you think you are?*

By this point, I was the sort of kid who revelled in adversity. I got a lot of strength through defining myself in opposition to the people around me. I don't actually think I'm better or brighter than anyone else but I definitely got some of my determination from this time, from a belligerent doggedness and desire to prove everyone wrong. I was just the wrong size. I was too much for that world, too big and too loud and I wanted more.

One prime example was when a DT (design and technology) teacher pulled me aside in the corridor between lessons. *What's yer backup plan for when you don't get into Oxford?* I was confused. He explained that he was doing a full school assembly and wanted to use me as an example of why it was important to have an alternative set of goals. He wanted to stand up in front of everyone and say look she's clever but even she is prepared to not get what she wants. I couldn't believe it. I was furious. I told him *There is no backup plan.* He didn't do the assembly.

This was all well and good but it did mean I had to follow through. I felt the weight of how much I had to prove myself. When you decide that you want to go against the grain and that you want something more, you'd better manage it. Otherwise you become the joke. When I collected my AS results, it was imperative that I got As across the board. There was a general consensus that I did not need to worry. I did all the work. I had continued to wake up at six before school. I felt like I couldn't fit any more work into the day. It also just so happened that the grades were released on my seventeenth birthday. The only gift I was bothered about was the marks.

It was the first time in my life that I had truly failed. I had managed to do very well in classics but everything else was way off the mark. I couldn't understand it. I stared at the paper, surrounded by everyone else, panicking. Nobody in my year had done very well. But I had dropped two, three, four grades. I had done everything I possibly could and it wasn't enough.

My mum had waited in the car. I slammed the door closed and in the confines of the Ford Focus I melted into a state of delirium. I was never going to manage it. I was stupid. I was going to be stuck here for the rest of my life.

The remainder of the summer was a pit. After the initial frenzy, I settled into a heavy cloud. I just didn't know who I was any more. If I wasn't a nerd who did well in exams, who was I? I went to a couple of parties and after the last one I was sick in the back of my parents' car. I had never been so sad. Mum and Dad said we'd make a plan. They put me in bed next to my brother with a bucket. I don't think Cas slept very well; he kept checking I wasn't going to choke on my vomit.

Any saying about failure is a wonderful cliché. It never makes the blow any easier. But for me, after that first earth shattering, I learnt that you survive it. I have also since learnt that failures don't stop coming. Much like hiccups and murders in *Poirot,* it's never just the one.

The start of a new school year was a public humiliation, walking in and seeing everyone looking at me. And they knew and cared. This sounds like a high school movie, with our protagonist walking in and everything juddering into slow motion. But in the first week of September, I walked into the sixth-form common room and felt every pair of eyes track me. My school was tiny, we all made it our business to ensure that the limited amount of information was well disseminated. I couldn't complain that I was the centre of attention because I love gossip. One must accept that sometimes you are the gossip.

But my parents and I had sat down and made the plan. I dropped English – my worst grades (D + E). I would have to re-sit the entirety of history AS and half of my French papers. I would still apply to Oxford. I just had to make sure everything else in my application was so outstandingly good they had to take me seriously. My essays were already solid because they were classics ones. My personal statement was fire. It wove in all the books I had read while focusing on my favourite idea that the greatest thing about classics was that it would be transformed and changed and adapted over and over again. Did it start with a quote? Of course it did, this was 2010 and the old *open with a quote* had just been invented. I had been writing and redrafting for the last six months. Mr Hussain and Mrs Wilson made sure that I had a great reference.

By some miracle, I did get an invite to interview despite the grades. That is more to do with the fact that not that many people want to study old dead languages and pots. But I did. Prepared to my eyeballs, I reread the books I had mentioned in my application. I packed carefully selected outfits into an old brown leather suitcase I bought myself for the occasion. Like every outsider, I put myself in a uniform. Overdressed, in vintage clothes, Mary Janes and a statement hat, I arrived in Evelyn Waugh-inspired drag.

Oxford is made up of colleges, which are bit like houses in Hogwarts. You apply to a college not just

the university. I had chosen Magdalen, which is pro-
nounced Maud-lin – my mother warned me ahead of
time. The Internet is a wonderful thing. I had decided
that if I was going to try to smuggle myself into this
university, I might as well heist myself into the most
majestic place I could find. Magdalen has its own deer
park. That seemed impressive to me, like a posh under-
stated zoo.

I flung the suitcase onto the bed in the room I
was staying in. I hung up my clothes. I sat down and
practised the breathing technique my mum had found
on YouTube. Four seconds in, hold for four seconds,
out for six, hold for six and repeat.

Before my first interview, I was shaking like a
shitting dog. The breathing helped. I had to be clever
and charming and keen. I just needed to be myself.
The first interview was with three old white men. I
was prepared for all the horror-story questions. You

know, *what was Augustus' favourite breakfast?* But they didn't do that at all. It was very kind and a little bit cruel. *What do you want to talk about?* The one question it had never crossed my mind they might have asked.

I left the first interview very confident. I had made them laugh. I had remembered lots of my reading and, most of all, I enjoyed it. Over the next few days, I had six more interviews at different colleges. None quite as successful as the first. In one, I was asked to put several pieces of ancient pot in chronological order. In another, we talked about grammar. The penultimate one was the worst. I was sent to another college and the tutor was wearing a drug-rug jumper which confused me. He asked me why I thought I deserved to get into Oxford with my grades. I welled up and through hyperventilating breaths tried to explain I'd only had a bad set of exams.

The last interview was at a college I had thought was single sex. It turned out that it had started accepting men, too. I was excited, one of the tutors was the pioneer in modern interpretations of classical works, which was my favourite. I was interviewed by three women on a low sofa. Midway through I had a mind-blank and I could feel them being generous. I thought it was pity.

After it was all done, I called my dad who drove all the way down to Oxford to pick me up. I cried the whole way home. I can't imagine it was quite the father-daughter road trip he had pictured.

My parents now talk about how they didn't sleep a lot during this time period. Mum thought it was an early menopause but it was actually stress on my behalf. They were terrified that I wouldn't manage it. It is hard to have faith in institutions that you have no experience with or that are ultimately exclusionary. I was scared too, but really my parents carried the heaviest burden.

In those days, they tried to let you know about the offers before Christmas. And they did it by letter. It was the last snowy December I remember, and the post was delayed. Other people had been getting their letters, according to forums on the Student Room. We went for a walk as some form of delay and distraction from what felt like impending doom. There was a letter waiting for me on my return. The envelope was stamped with the St Hilda's crest. That was the college with the women on the sofa. I opened it – an offer dependant on three As. Those three had decided to take a chance on me. We all cried with relief.

I rang the school to let them know. The headmistress told me that *I must have misread the letter.*

Now it was just the little matter of the grades. My parents found me a history tutor – Tracey. She was a PhD student whose speciality was Disney and fascism. She was bubbly and wore a lot of Mickey Mouse-emblazoned jumpers. She got equally excited talking about the intricacies of the Nazi government and the newest additions to the princesses. To support herself through her studies she worked in the Disney Store in the shopping centre and she came round our house on a Sunday morning. She coached me in exam techniques. I wrote essay plan after essay plan. I realised that I had never before been shown what an essay was supposed to look like. That there were ways of structuring my writing to hit exam criteria. I had always just gone in and tried to write as much information as possible on a page. Now I saw that I had been working hard but not effectively. I hadn't known there were rules.

I also started getting up even earlier in the morning, this time sneaking in two hours before school. What little social life I had before was put on hold. I promised myself that I could have fun after all this hard work. With or without the grades, I had the rest of my life to go out. Being a teenager is shit anyway, I told myself.

Most of all, I was terribly lonely. I felt isolated from the rest of the world. What few friends I had had gone to university the year before or were far away.

I spent a lot of time thinking about the future, taking each individual day at a time. I learnt my dates for history and my French grammar, but mainly I built the foundations of my work ethic. I sewed an ability to be alone into the fabric of who I am. I knew it wouldn't be like this forever. Things would change.

I took what comfort I could from myths and the classical texts I read – Sappho, especially. Most of the fragments of her poetry we have because someone found them in an ancient dump site. That's just like me, I thought. I was lost, fragmented and lucky.

It is the ultimate relief – the thought that for thousands of years we have felt love and anger and desperation. One of the fragments (thirty-eight) just reads *You burn me*. It is tiny little messages from the past and the future coming to tell you that you aren't alone, that we all look at the same stars and wonder what the fuck is going on. The sort of words that make you forget time and remember eternity.

I also kept up my regular visits to the library, usually with my dad who would order things weekly. That's the thing about writers, we are a group of lonely, isolated freaks and often that's what loads of books are about. So it is impossible not to feel a part of some great cult when you read. It is transformative.

Time swung around as it always does. I sat my A-levels. As I left the room I felt none the wiser. I could have smashed them or I could have fucked it all up. We knew that I couldn't spend the whole summer just waiting for the results, so I went off to Rome to au pair some Italian children that a relative knew.

Tension is a powerful thing. The pulling of multiple possibilities creates an odd nervous energy. The only thing I knew for certain was that something was around the corner. It felt like there were only two possible outcomes: either I would jump and fly or I would step out and plummet off the precipice. But that is being a teenager for you, very little nuance. What I was thankful for was that something was about to happen and my life was about to change beyond what I could imagine.

I have always bragged about my ability to sleep anywhere and any time. As long as I have something resembling two out of three of dark, warmth or quiet, I can drop off. But I think that actually I massively overcompensate for the fact that for long stretches at a time I am struck by terror. I can nap during the day because at night I am possessed by psychedelic dreams and an anxious stranglehold. This started when I was waiting for my final A-level results. Every time I slept, I dreamt about picking up my grades. In these dreams, half the time I failed miserably and the other half I succeeded. I believe it was my brain putting me through a rehearsal process to ensure that I could survive either outcome.

It worked. There was no way that I was recreating the previous year's humiliation. Bleary-eyed and petrified, I shakily rang and re-rang UCAS. When I got through, the woman on the end told me that she couldn't give me the grades. She could only tell me if my university offers had been confirmed, but that's all I cared about.

I cried, obviously. I'm not sure that I can express any emotion through anything but tears. I was crying so much that my dad, coming out of the shower, heard me and ran upstairs with a hand towel round his waist. I had always thought that the bit in *Billy Elliot* where he gets into ballet school is a bit hammy. Why doesn't he just spit it out? But nobody could understand what I was saying because I was crying. *I did it, I did it, I made it, I got in.*

I went to collect my results from the school and saw how close I had been to the abyss. I got my required three As but only just, I had scraped by. I did it by one UMS mark – which is less than one mark in the actual exam. I felt the fragility of it all. Mrs Wilson wasn't there so I didn't have anyone to celebrate with. The headmistress just coldly said *You must be pleased.* They couldn't be happy for me because they had been wrong. The next day I turned eighteen. Then I packed.

Now, I know you have probably read the blurb. You know what is going to happen. In the next chapter I am about to discover something that at this moment is unimaginable and will unravel the fabric of who I think I am. I'm sorry to break the narrative wall briefly but I believe it is very important to be explicit.

This is not a story of an inspirational disabled person overcoming adversity through hard work. I am not prepared to take on that role or represent that. I was incredibly lucky to get into Oxford; I could so easily have not got those marks. When I reflect on this part in my particular story, all I can really think about are the people who weren't as lucky as I was. I want to be clear on my position that our current education system lets down too many people. It fails to help so many children with (and without) learning difficulties reach their full potential. The answer is not to demand that we work harder to smuggle ourselves through the system that does not want us. Trust me, we are already working so hard just to jump through the hoops you have falsely decided mark our intelligence. We should not be the collateral damage of a system that does not work.

CHAPTER 6

FITTING

The following weeks were a blur.

That first drive to Oxford was intense and significant. We swung into the edge of the city while our favourite Nina Simone album played. We were all singing at the top of our voices. I knew that it didn't really matter what Oxford was like because it had been about getting there. It was symbolic for us all, that we could sneak into the system. It meant that things could change.

It was October, but the sort of autumn where the summer leaves behind a little heat. I was the new kid again but this time everyone was in the same boat as me, at least that's what I thought. I was shown to my room by a bright sun-dressed girl in the year above who was already settled into this new world. It was welcoming.

Now, I was already quite prepared for the culture shock. I had read *Brideshead Revisited* years prior and I knew that I was entering into a world with new words and rules. The traditions were sewn into the fabric of the university. They were institutionalised to let everyone know that this was a hallowed, sacred place of learning – not like those *other* universities. At first, I bought into it.

Before I get going, I should explain some of those key things. As I have already mentioned Oxford and Cambridge are universities but they are split into smaller institutions within that called colleges.

Colleges are like little villages of 400 or so students split across many years and even into masters and doctorate students. Each college has a dining hall, common rooms and their own accommodation. Generally, your main contact time is with your college tutors on top of bigger university-wide faculty teaching like lectures and classes. The college system can be great – it splits the world into manageable bite-sized chunks. In theory, it should mean that you get more attention from your teaching staff and that you can have a tiny community. But it can also be insular and at its worst it has real small-village vibes.

Where I ended up was pretty special. St Hilda's isn't the sort of college you think of when you imagine Oxbridge. Not even one *Morse* spin-off has been filmed there. As it used to be a women-only college, it is relatively new. By new, I mean created in the twentieth century rather than being a medieval shrine to the Virgin Mary, or whatever the other colleges are. There were no quads (pointless squares of grass you can't walk on) or cloisters (those stone outdoor corridors you see in *Harry Potter*) or towers (big stone phalluses you can climb up). So in some ways one could be disappointed by not getting the postcard image of the oldest university in the country. But to be honest, I was just glad to be there, and as time went on I realised that not being in one of the older, more stuffy institutions was key to my happiness over the four years of my degree.

I liked that the dining room was a glorified canteen painted pink and that the food was so much better than at other colleges. The bar was student-run, and on Thursdays ran a wildly successful *Pound a Pint night!* The other students didn't seem to take themselves too seriously and our sports teams were nothing to brag about. The library was nice and there was a college cat, Teabag.

My room was everything I could have ever dreamt of. I learnt later that for some reason most of the other students hated the brutalist accommodation block I had been allocated. We were put in our rooms alphabetically, like a set of library books. It was the only listed building the college had and I could see why. My room looked onto the big beech tree which stood tall over the college like a guard. Concrete and wood make this trellised building really pop in contrast to the golden sandstone of the other buildings. The corridors inside the building looked like what I imaged 1970s cruise ships sported as their chic interiors. This image was only confirmed as the year went by and I stumbled home to the swaying passage after a fiver's worth of larger.

My dad was impressed by the Bridget Riley prints on the stairwell and by the fact I had a lift. I loved the self-contained room with its floor-to-ceiling window, single bed, sink and desk. It was a little paradise of my own, especially after my mum helped me put up the collection of postcards and vintage cigarette cards that she gave me for my eighteenth birthday.

After they left, I sat on my bed with the gingham duvet cover that I had originally slept under as a small child, and watched the autumnal sunset bathed in pride. It felt much more momentous than the rest of freshers' week. That consisted largely of repeated

conversations with people who I had no particular desire to talk to. I found it very difficult to drop the necessary guard that I had built to protect myself at school. Also, I genuinely had very little will to be liked by most of the people I encountered. I couldn't swallow down the feeling that I wasn't particularly a fit here either. Not because I didn't deserve to be there, but because I just hadn't clicked with anyone yet. It also probably didn't help that I'd never had hummus, pesto or Prosecco before.

This was merely compounded by the constant enquiry of *where did you go to school?* At first I thought it was just an inane conversation starter. But as the week progressed and I heard other people's responses, I twigged that there were famous schools other than just Eton. It made me sick that so many people had friends and acquaintances here. Some schools had sent half the year to Oxbridge. It was like this had been a viable option to them rather than some labour of impossibility come true. It really undermined the illusion of meritocracy and it made me furious.

Oxford was nothing like Batley; I had hoped for that. But there were unexpected things that made me very uncomfortable. It was so white. I was used to my classes and shops and buses having women wearing niqabs and the streets busy for Friday night prayers. Then I discovered my room had been allocated a weekly cleaner who would hoover and empty my bins. These *scouts* are an Oxford institution, but I couldn't stand it (and I hate hoovering and emptying my bins). I didn't understand why. It was not even remotely normal to me.

I have never been one for having a chip on my shoulder. Mainly, as I am aware of how lucky I am. I have the ultimate privilege of the unwavering support of my parents and that I mostly like who I am. But that first year at Oxford made me wrathful and I revelled in crossing lines. I made inappropriate jokes and swore like a sailor. I was challenging the lovely girls from the home counties and the rugby boys to try to like me. I openly laughed when I was introduced to a Benedict (Bens in my world were Benjamins) and horrified when I met two more. There is one thing I do (partially) regret; my neighbour kept walking into my room unannounced and wanting to have cups of tea and chats. After the third occasion, I said *Just because our surnames start with the same letter doesn't mean that we're going to be friends.* That was cruel. I knew it was at the time, but sometimes I can be a dick and I wanted to be left alone.

The anger came from feeling as isolated as in Batley. The only solution to that kind of solitude is to find people that make you feel less alone in the world, even if it is just momentary. Oxford, however, did introduce me to many kindred spirits. Luckily for me, I didn't have to rely on our alphabetised living arrangements for my friends.

It is hard to say whether it was my own latent homosexuality that drew me to the androgynous figure. But like attracts like. I saw someone that was the spit of the cover of my favourite Enid Blyton book, *The Naughtiest Girl in the School*. It had been my favourite because it was my mum's favourite she had actually lived up to that accolade in her own girls' school. But here, in the auditorium of St Hilda's college, was that girl with the mop of dark curls, but her school uniform consisted of all-black Nike Airs and about three gold chains. I knew instantly that I had seen my best friend, and Rachel Watkeys Dowie didn't really have much to say about the situation.

RACHEL

The wild thing is that I was right. She was raised by artists. When I asked my parents what class we were, my mum had said we were *No Class*. Which is sort of right and sort of wrong. *We are Bohemians*; culturally rich and very cash poor. I hadn't ever met someone else like that before, and during the first few days of Oxford it felt like maybe I wasn't going to here, either. But as I got to know Rachel it was impossible not to see the similarities. We had got to Oxford, defying the expectations of our teachers. We had younger brothers who we loved to excess, and our parents had tried to raise us to question society's norms of how we are supposed to be.

But unlike me, Rachel is beloved by all. She flourished in this world and used her boisterous South London charm to woo the various groups that had already started to form in the first few weeks of term. Rachel was popular and flitted in and out. Of course, I was jealous. Rach jokes that in the photos of this first year, I am always scowling and she is always smoking. She used her difference to seduce, whereas I think I used mine to push back. But I had decided she was my friend and we've basically stuck together in some way or another since.

That first year, Rach spent a lot of time flirting with various groups and I made one other very close friend. Olivia was from Stoke, which sounded as shit as Batley and she seemed just as angry as I was. We were thick as thieves. She studied Japanology, which I think I instantly regretted not studying the moment I realised it was an option. Cas and I had spent much of our teenage years saving up for manga volumes and Naruto-running round the house. Olivia and I instantly bonded when she dressed up as Sailor Moon in freshers' week. She felt like the first proper friend I had ever had. She liked that I was belligerent and silly and ridiculous.

The work started straight away. There was no grace period; we were set essays in the first few days of arrival. This started the pattern for the following four years: an endless sequence of reading, essay writing and then tutes. Tutorials (or tutes if you're nasty) are hour-long meetings with your tutors where you discuss the week's topic such as: free will in the *Iliad*, column

development in temples, erect penises as comic devices in political comedy, and other upstanding topics like that. Often you will have one or two other students in the room with you, but you could also frequently find yourself alone with the world's specialist on Athenian comedy in the fifth century BC, for example. Many people are intimidated by this very thought. But I relished it. The best decision I made before I arrived at university was to resolve to have fun. I had no intention of being the cleverest because I knew that would be an impossible task. So when I went into tutorials, I asked difficult questions and thought on the spot. I had a lot of fun and got a lot wrong.

On the other hand, writing essays was a different thing altogether. I would read hundreds of pages and then try to construct some argument. But as I wrote, new ideas would sidetrack me. I would lose interest in certain threads and I would shoehorn in the information I had found on the reading list. I would deliver my essay and for those tutes where I was required to, I would read it out loud and edit it as I spoke. The words on the page seemingly unrecognisable from what I had thought I had written.

I was lucky, my tutors were not too bothered about grades. For the many essays they asked of me, they didn't put a mark at the top. This built the atmosphere that the most important thing was the ideas and the discussion.

Unlike most university students in the country, I still had early morning classes. Every morning at nine I would have to drag myself to my Ancient Greek lesson. It was headed by a formidable Italian woman who was deeply unimpressed by her new cohort. *How did you get into Oxford, you're stupid!* I liked her a lot; the harshness felt just like a cheeky challenge. By the end of the term she baked us a cake each week and still called us stupid. I found learning the language tricky. I did all the work set me

α A
β B
γ Γ
δ Δ
ε E
ζ Z
η H
θ Θ
ι I
κ K
λ Λ
μ M
ν N
ξ Ξ
ο O
π Π
ρ P
σ Σ
τ T
υ Υ
φ Φ
χ X
ψ Ψ
ω Ω

and nothing more because it was already a mountain…
I had learnt the Greek alphabet in advance, but the
speed at which we moved through the tenses and
grammar was impressive. Well, I'm impressed at those
who managed to keep up. I did the homework and met
deadlines but, if I'm quite honest, I would still trip
over the new alphabet. The equivalent of r looks like
a p, and I struggled to fit in all the new vocabulary.
I probably needed twice the amount of time to catch
up but with essays and socialising and annoying sleep
dependency there was never enough time.

I thought I would meet at least a couple of geniuses
in Oxford. I really had bought the propaganda. But let
me assure you, there isn't really such a thing as a genius.
Even if there is, it is a dangerous role to put on someone
or to take on yourself because the invisible label in
front of genius is 'doomed'. I am happily willing to
take on the label of 'lucky' idiot. I did meet some very
academic people, some who found the languages easy
or were apparently sublime mathematicians but also
lots of them couldn't cook or tie their laces. Trust me
when I say there are many different types of intelligence
and education. Nobody has them all. Maybe you're a
social charmer who can read any room with no formal
education or perhaps you're a physics professor who
has to wear Velcro shoes and can't read an analogue
clock – there really shouldn't be a hierarchy of these
skills. One is not *cleverer* than the other.

That first year was a real cocktail. Not like a delicious pina colada but more like how a dirty pint is technically a cocktail. Every individual part was in itself important and tasty but combined it was just a mess. I wasn't unhappy; in fact I was over the moon just to be in Oxford. I was thirsty for the real world, which is ironic because Oxford is not the real world. But I had a culture shock. I couldn't quite square my term time with the time I had to spend at home in the holidays. I was exhausted from the work and the parties. Then I would go back to Batley and remember that most people didn't live the way I did at university, with three meals a day cooked for you. I pushed a lot of the discomfort aside and tried to focus on my excitement for this new world that made me feel like I was full of potential.

My accent disappeared too. I didn't do it on purpose. I was doing a lot of auditioning for plays in Oxford and feeling like I wasn't welcome or that the roles that were on offer were either for pretty posh girls or girls willing to play posh old ladies. The one exception was when I auditioned for John Godber's *Teechers*. He's from Hull and his plays tend to require regional accents. I shared my audition with a girl who was very keen to tell me she had done a year at LAMDA. She warmed up loudly and I shivered in my coat with cold and nerves as the draught lapped up the stone corridor. In the room, the director asked if we could do the accent. *I can do just a general rough working-class voice*, LAMDA girl bragged. I was so angry and so relieved in one. I got the part and she didn't. However, she went on to get all the pretty posh-girl roles for the following three years. That was just one of the messages Oxford sent me about my voice.

The second message I received even louder and clearer. I was asked to go to an alumni event. It was hosted in the Houses of Parliament and there was free booze. I dressed up in a black velvet dress from a vintage shop; in the light you could see green roses shine in the fabric. I really looked the part as I swanned into the room filled with ex-students. There were lots of old white ladies. Most were very formidable and successful. I fell into conversation with one who was in her seventies and who had studied classics half a century ago. I was explaining to her the new course I was on where you could learn Latin and Greek from scratch. She kept tutting at me. I changed the topic. I tried to inspire her with talk of Euripides. She interrupted me. *Really, I can't listen to you speak a word more. Stop saying 'like'. You sound dreadful. Nobody will ever take you seriously with a voice like that. Stop crying. I'm helping you. Young women like you sound like idiots.* I swiftly ran to the toilets.

Now people ask, *So where's your accent? You don't sound northern.* You can be sure as shit they have the same innocuous nothing voice. I dismiss it, joking that a posh university bashed it out of me. It is easier to credit the loss of my accent to just that one thing and not a long accumulation of experiences outside the county where what I said and how I said it was repeated back to me over and over again. It's easier than to say I felt unwelcome or that I felt like I had to squash it out so that I could fit in. How else could I see myself in that space with my voice? Now it feels like a price I had to pay to leave Batley.

It's still there, just a little bit if you listen. My A's are flat and to's are t's. *Ah'll see ya ten-tuh-two.* When I'm angry or a pint down, it tumbles out as strong as ever. It makes me happy to hear that it didn't get completely trampled out. I think about how on earth do I get it back – do I consciously put it back on? But it's not a hat I can just don. That would make it feel like a costume, when it's so much more complicated than that. In many ways I got what I wanted. I wanted to leave, I didn't want my future tied to that one place forever. But I certainly didn't want to erase my past and my roots and my voice in the process.

I was grappling with all of that in the first year. But I went into the second year feeling a bit more confident. I had some big exams coming up and I had a student house so I could stay in Oxford outside term time. It felt like maybe I could solidify my place in this new world rather than flip-flopping between the two places.

My mum drove me to my new house on her own because Dad was away. I was the first one to move in. I was anxious about it as I had to arrange my housemates early the previous year; Rachel was one of them but I wasn't close to the other three girls. Olivia was in Japan on her year abroad but I was planning to go out and visit her in one of the holidays. I was worried about being even more lonely without my friend. After we had set up my room, Mum disappeared off leaving me in this strange house alone.

I started making myself some haute cuisine – probably some sort of pasta or egg-based dish on the electric hob. The new kitchen was weird. It had fake wood panelling, which gave it a 1970s ski chalet vibe. I was engrossed in thinking about this new environment when I tripped up and fell forward, steadying myself with my right hand. I didn't see as I flew head first that my hand was heading towards the hob. As I pulled my hand away I could smell the burning skin. I called my mum, now halfway up the M1, with my hand under the cold tap. We didn't have the Internet installed yet so I had Cas read the NHS advice page down the phone to me: *if the burn is larger than the palm of your hand, go to your local A&E department.* Well, at least I had an accurate measure of the blister size. That night I lay in my new bed with my hand in a bowl of water and cried. I'm afraid to say that it really set the tone for that second year.

The house filled up with my housemates and I continued to feel alone. A classmate ripped me apart for being excited about buying a new mobile phone. *You're so privileged you don't understand.* It was my second ever phone and later I went to her house and met her mother the high court judge and realised that the guilt was *maybe* misplaced. I didn't hear from Olivia for months. Rachel got her first girlfriend, which meant I didn't see her much. My bike kept breaking and my exams were fast approaching. One of my housemates wouldn't let me put on the heating and my windows weren't sealed properly so the room was well ventilated. I ended up sleeping in the fur coat I had bought to look the part at balls, which felt more *Withnail and I* than I had anticipated.

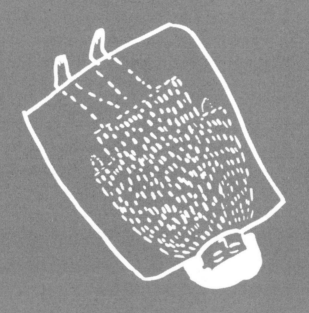

Eventually, I got an email from Olivia. She evidently was also not in a good place. But she said she no longer wanted to be my friend, that I was negative and saw the worst in people and that it was poisonous. It was like she had used all the things I had told her in confidence that I hated about myself to destroy me. Together, we had always said that maybe the rest of the world needed to be better but here she was telling me that I was the problem. This was completely unforeseen. She had played a key part in my navigation of Oxford. She had felt as much of an outsider as me and I had been deeply touched by her presence in my life.

It is impossible not to take such a comment to heart when it comes from someone you love. I was flooded and drowning. All the things that I had hidden away in deep crevices of my being paraded up into focus. Like a monkey with a cymbal bashing my brain cried out *lethal! polluting! vicious! toxic! noxious! corruptive! viperous!* I didn't know I knew so many synonyms and that I was capable of weaponising my vocabulary against myself so brutally.

I tried my best to just hold it all far away from me for as long as possible. *If it gets me*, I thought, *I am going to die.* I wasn't going to kill myself but I was pretty certain I was going to get hit by a bus while cycling, maybe. It was that terrifying feeling of impending doom and, even more scarily, the idea that I might do something to speed up the inevitable. I cried on Rachel a lot. The sky was low and had the quality of office ceiling tiles. I called my parents and asked them to come get me, weeks before I had planned. *She broke your heart*, said Mum and I let myself be eaten by the sadness. It didn't kill me. The thought of how much it was going to hurt was worse than just feeling the loss.

The next term heralded my first big exams at Oxford. They're called Mods and they're famously (apparently – I didn't know before, either) gruelling. *Hardest exams in the world tied with the Chinese civil service ones until they made those easier last year*, I once heard someone claim. I googled the Chinese civil service exams only to find out that they were in place from the Zhou dynasty (1067-ish) to the end of imperialism in China (1911) so I assumed that someone was talking out of their arse, not an uncommon thing in the dreaming spires. I wasn't too worried because I had sort of kept up with my work, I never handed in stuff late and I wrote the essays. I just needed to revise. So as I tried to recover from what I thought might have been depression and now recognise as grief, I spent hours in the library. I would try to read and make notes and not cry too openly. Funnily enough, it felt like most people in the library, with or without exams, seemed to be doing the same thing.

The exams came round and we had to sit eleven three-hour exams in eight days. In Oxford, another one of the weird traditions is that you have to sit exams in a uniform called subfusc, which is essentially a black-and-white costume – white shirt, black tie or ribbon and black skirt or trousers; oh, and a gown. You

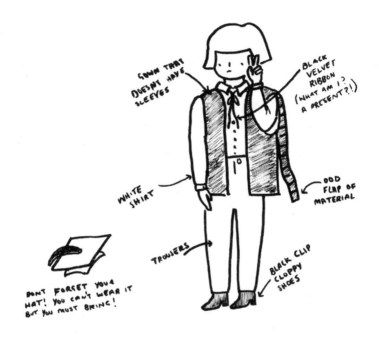

GOWN THAT DOESNT HAVE SLEEVES

BLACK VELVET RIBBON (WHAT AM I? A PRESENT?!)

WHITE SHIRT

ODD FLAP OF MATERIAL

TROUSERS

BLACK CLIP CLOPPY SHOES

DONT FORGET YOUR HAT! YOU CAN'T WEAR IT BUT YOU MUST BRING!

sit the exams in the building where humanities lectures are held, called Examination Schools. The 400 people doing your subject are herded up marble staircases into these beautiful high-ceilinged rooms. Then, at the end of the exams you get trashed, which sounds like the binge drinking you would expect at every university but *trashing* is when your friends cover you in shaving foam and confetti and booze.

Before the exams, I had thought these were great symbols – like arming yourself before war and the catharsis of mess. But half an hour into my first paper on the *Iliad*, I was uncomfortable and the echoey room was draughty and noisy. When I finished all my exams I exited only to find that nobody had come to trash me. *Bloody traditions*, I muttered to myself as I skulked off to the pub with my fellow classicists, my drab clothes still pristine. I watched in amazement as one of the boys from St Hilda's downed a pint of Guinness, and realised that we all probably hadn't had the most fun in Exam Schools. I wondered who exactly benefitted from all the rigmarole.

I had ticked off each exam. They were hard, obviously, and I was still manically writing to the last minute and not having time to check through, let alone really even think. In one I was required to translate a passage from English into Ancient Greek, which is a ridiculous thing to ask someone to do. Translating the other way round is, yes, a specialist skill but at least has a point. The only possible reason to do it the other way round might be if you found yourself in a time-travel rom-com scenario (possible titles – *Bacchus to the Future, You were never really Hera, There's no place like Homer*).

I had revised for this exam but found myself struggling to recall anything I had learnt over the last year and a half. The only foreign language I could think of was French (which I had studied for A-level but I wouldn't say I was fluent by any stretch of the imagination). I thought I was writing in Ancient Greek but when I got my results back I realised I couldn't have been. I failed that exam so badly that I must have been writing in French but in the Greek alphabet. μερδε.

Now, failing my second set of exams still sucked. But this time, it was mainly just the shame. I didn't need the grades for anything in particular but I was used to the idea of doing well. I emailed my tutors who assured me that I didn't have to retake the failed papers because I'd managed to wangle a 2:2 overall. *I know you must be disappointed but they don't count so please don't worry about it,* Dr Kearns replied. Now I see how lucky I was, lots of other tutors would be annoyed and think about their college rankings, but not mine.

I had just picked my papers for the second half of my degree, opting perhaps foolishly to learn Latin from scratch after the *overwhelming success* of my Greek papers. But I wanted to be able to translate both classical languages and I had my heart set on the Ovid paper for some reason. I don't like giving up, unless it's sports related and in that case I don't even really get started. We just carried on with tutorials and essays and reading and language classes. I was so used to the seemingly random highs and lows of my academic life. This was normal for me. I concluded that I must just be erratic.

At the end of summer term (they call it Trinity, and not because they love *The Matrix* but because of tradition) things were looking up. It was sunny, I was about to move into a rad flat with cool people and I was flirting with a girl who would soon become my first girlfriend. I went to go have my termly report reading and Dr Kearns had written *I suspect there might be some undiagnosed dyslexia here.* I sat on the low sofa where I had been interviewed two and a half years previously, and I began to cry and panic. My tutor looked alarmed but I can assure you she wasn't as alarmed as I was.

CHAPTER 7

FINDING

The first thing I thought as I left the room was that it was *impossible – I can read. I bloody love reading. So I can't be dyslexic. I'm smart. There's nothing wrong with me. She's wrong.*

My internal monologue was shouting and denying any possibility of having a learning difficulty with such fervour that I knew that something was up. Slowly, as I walked along the river to the hidden bench under a flowering tree, I let those thoughts drop for a few moments. I sat there watching the water flow and remembered all the times I had struggled. Then a new feeling emerged, a hope. Maybe it would explain all the places in which my brain seemed to trip, stick and judder like an old scratched CD. But even the thought of the label hurt my ego. I didn't know what it meant to be dyslexic but when I heard people make mention of it, it was with a tone of pity or excuse or despair.

I had no facts, just the impression that this was a bad thing that I should be ashamed of.

I called my parents on that bench. They were expecting me – I always called them after my report readings. They began to list all the possible evidence: failed exams, late learning to write, struggling with spelling, messy handwriting, occasional comments from early teachers. But there were two counters – *but you always loved reading* (this seemed like concrete evidence to us all) and *we were told you were tested in school and nothing came up.*

I wracked my brains. Had I been tested? I had no recollection of any test presented to me as one for dyslexia. We had been made to sit something in the school's IT room which we were told was to test our raw ability and predict what sort of level we should be working at. Perhaps that was some hidden test, but nothing had come out of it.

It was the last day of term, which meant that the undergraduate part of the university was about to close up for the summer. I had been informed that the next steps I had to take involved getting in contact with the Disability Advisory Service (DAS) who were a university-wide organisation. I sent them an email that day and then celebrated the end of the year with my friends.

At a party in the bar, I drank a lot of vodka, which like all my experiences with the spirit, made me vomit. Though, this time, it was on the girl I had been flirting with for the previous eight weeks. We had kissed for the first time and gone back to her room. The next thing I knew it was 4 a.m. and I was not at home. I looked about the unknown location and put what little shaky evidence I had in my brain cobbled together and ran. I hastily wrote my phone number on a piece of paper and left it on Martha's bedside table. I trekked up Cowley Road to my sad room and crawled into bed to hide from the world. *Well*, I thought to myself, *thank god I don't remember anything more of that...*

The next morning, I woke up to the worst hangover of my life. It was colossal, like my head was being squeezed between the thighs of one of the Williams sisters (preferably Venus, just for the classical name), but not in a sexy way. I was certain that I would be sick again and I spent all the possible strength I had restraining myself from hurling chunks. With hindsight I should have just let myself vomit into oblivion – it would have made me feel better, but pride hurts. Rachel knocked gleefully on my door and peered in with a delighted grin.

I had spent the first two years of my time at university managing to pretty steadily remain composed. Even to the early morning classes, I would turn up on time, showered and with my makeup on – especially on the occasions when I had got little sleep and I was still drunk. I prided myself on being pretty unshakable – fun, but knowing my own limits. I had helped friends when they had crossed the line, I had put girls I barely knew into bed after helping them vomit in the shared toilet, and I was not above giving people water and pretending it was booze.

Rachel was wilder than me but was not the sort of person who needed looking after like that. She had once had to come find me down the Cowley Road after an argument with some little shit, but in her words – *nothing as fun as this*. Who doesn't enjoy seeing people's composure shaken a little. Especially when it's tied to some gay gossip. Rachel had my phone – which I had managed to leave in Martha's room, along with my bra. Here I was in bed sick as a pig and unravelling at the edges. Rachel loves

DID YOU FORGET SOMETHING?

seeing me out of control like that and she is always the first person to be invited in when it happens because, well, she reminds me that it can be fun to be a mess. *It's exciting! Something is happening.*

The rest of the day in bed, I flip-flopped between mortification about my own behaviour from the previous night and what my report had said.

Days later, and just about recovered, I had to take myself to the Disability Advisory Service for an initial consultation. The DAS was in an odd little newly built square in Oxford. I arrived stupidly early because I was worried about getting lost and becoming late. After thirty minutes in the waiting room, I was shown to my appointment with a young guy called Danny. Danny was exactly everything I had expected. He was young, wearing a t-shirt and his wrists were adorned with wooden beads, friendship bracelets and festival bands. In his office he had a poster which read: *If only we put as much money into the war on poverty as we do the war on terror.* Which I agreed with but also I felt annoyed that he was such a cliché. He made me go through a list with him – *did I have to reread passages for information; did I learn to read late; would people describe me as clumsy; do you struggle with structuring essays?*

Yes, yes, yes, yes, I said in the smallest voice I have.

He booked me in for a proper assessment, a long one with a specialist. This was just the first hoop to jump through, a pre-assessment. I would need to meet with an educational psychologist. It would be free but I needed to fill out some forms. He helped me fill them in and, as he did, I realised how much I hated having to put my name and address into the little boxes, that with him it took no time at all but if I had been home, that form would have sat on my cluttered desk demanding to be filled in but I would have taken a day just to write down information that I knew. *Uh oh.*

My assessment was on my last day in Oxford before my lease ended and I went up north for the summer holidays, and so Mum and Cas were down to help me move. They wandered around Oxford while I disappeared for three and a half hours. My educational psychologist was even more of a cliché than Danny. She was a small middle-aged woman who whispered. She offered me a green tea but all I wanted was for her to bloody speak up.

In the weeks prior to the assessment I had been fantasising about how great having the extra help would be. I felt that it would transform my experience at university and in the exams. There are always rumours in the air that some people fake it in their assessment – pretend to be unable to do the activities. It would be completely disingenuous of me to say I didn't think about it – not just once or twice, even as I walked into the room. But I had decided it would be A) morally wrong (obviously) and B) a disservice to myself because I needed to know the truth. Plus, I always try my hardest, it's one of the things I have always liked about myself and I wasn't going to stop here.

It all turned out to be irrelevant because the sets of exercises she gave me to do were hard. I was trying my best and I knew I wasn't getting it right. She read lists of numbers to me and asked me to repeat them back. I couldn't do more than three without getting muddled. She did word associations... for example: *Sistine Chapel.*

Er, I know this one, er, Michael, er, Angelo.
The Thinker.
I definitely know this one. My Granddad likes it. No, don't move on. It's there [taps head] R... R... RODIN.

Next were the blocks. It felt incredibly infantilising. You had to put different prisms and cubes into the shape shown on a card, and quickly. It was like having to put a piece of Ikea furniture up without the instructions. By the last one I felt like throwing each block piece out of the window one by one while making intense eye contact with the woman. But it was pointless, I knew she'd just write that down on her little clipboard and get out another set.

I slowly began to realise that it wasn't that I was stupid, it was that my brain seemed to have an awesome delay. It culminated in the last exercise where I had to read a passage aloud. I managed without a hitch. Sort of. Until she asked me some comprehension questions about what I had read. I couldn't answer a single one. I had just read it out loud, I hadn't struggled to sound out the words. But not one bit of information of the twenty lines had been absorbed by my brain. That's when I knew, there was absolutely no doubt in my mind that I had at least dyslexia.

It felt like I had been possessed. That I had been going through all the motions all this time in Oxford. Opening books and looking at the words and making notes and writing essays but nothing had actually been reaching me. I had been relying on the original passages, the stories and the easier secondary texts for a year and a half. Not because I was lazy or tired but because my brain wasn't getting the support from me it needed.

Right at the end of the assessment, three hours down, I was in a state of heightened panic. *When you read do the words move round on the page?* What a ridiculous question, I thought. I think I'd bloody notice if I was trying to read and the letters were doing a can-can in front of me. If that was the case I'd never be able to read, and I love reading. My lifejacket was back.

I just said, *No, I don't think so.* But she asked me to try an overlay. I picked a shade – parrot green, to humour her. But when I put it on the passage I wanted to jump into a wood chipper. Because it did make a difference. It wasn't that the words had been dancing around before, it was that they were noisy. Each one begging to be read, shaking and insisting that they were the important bit. With this bit of plastic, it quietened down the pulsing and the brightness of the page didn't speckle my eyes like sun spots.

I left the room desolate. I joined Wizzy and Cas. We went for the worst Philly cheese sub I've ever had, not just because I was upset, it was bad food and that made me feel even worse. As I stared at the congealed onions and the orange American plastic cheese, I was wrecked. How on earth did this happen to me?

Know yourself. That was the one thing I always came back to in moments of despair. When I was knackered and feeling shit, I would take myself home and eat nice food and go to bed. If I was sad, I would try to look at myself and what had happened around me to work out why and what I could change. But I had failed to do this in terms of my brain and how I thought. It shook me. I could logically understand it. It is impossible to know how other people see the world. As a young child I loved thinking about how we could all see blue as different colours but that we all called it the same thing. The Ancient Greeks love calling the sea *wine dark*, which I loved because it represented that we culturally see and understand the world in different ways. But even so, I couldn't *understand*. I could not grasp it.

It was undoubtedly a pivotal moment. Like the ground giving way beneath you and swinging to reveal a whole new self. All of those dark thoughts which sat behind my ears now swam forward with a vengeance. I had always suspected that I wasn't actually very clever, that I was just hard working. Now, it appeared that I had the evidence to support that feeling.

My full assessment report arrived in my inbox. I had spent the weeks between the assessment flailing between a desire to be 'normal' and a desperate need to be recognised and seen. The report stated that I was dyslexic and dyspraxic. It also placed me in the top 1 per cent of the population for verbal ability. In the assessment, the educational psychologist had tried to explain that she was looking for a disparity in ability. Reading the twenty-five-page document, I began to understand what that meant. There were charts and percentages placing my scores against an average. In certain things, I was exceptional and in others I was in the bottom 10 per cent. My weaknesses were largely centred in trying to recall information rapidly and sight reading. It made me feel better to realise that those scary unspellable words, dyslexia and dyspraxia, were really just names for the gap between the things I was good at and my weaknesses.

The report also stated I needed extra time and a laptop in exams. It called for further support during my studies, including technology to help and one-to-one sessions with a specialist. I forwarded the report to my parents and the tutor who had flagged the possibility of having SpLDs.

That summer I went to my first Pride and reconnected with the girl I vomited on, Martha. She returned my bra and we began a long courtship of letters and emails when she went to Princeton for a term. It is odd to reflect on that period and how much writing I must have been doing without being self-conscious about it. We wrote to each other for months. When I started back at university for my third year, every essay I wrote felt full of glaring errors. I could see every mistake, which before I would have simply skimmed over and pushed aside as a result of exhaustion or laziness. But now it felt like I had gotten worse. But in those letters to Martha, we exchanged poems and I penned long missives about my day and all the fresh thoughts that come with a first love. I never felt stupid when I wrote to her. But perhaps that is the blindness that comes with an outpour of emotion. Now I think it was also a reminder that writing is a joy when you don't use it as a stick to beat yourself with.

But at the same point in time, in the library, I would reread the same page of critical theory over and over, each repetition lending no further clarity. In fact, I began to see the mechanics of how I read. It was terrifying. The assessor had pointed out to me at the time that I must have had an extraordinary set of coping mechanisms in order to remain undiagnosed for this long. Looking at those mechanisms was like looking behind the screen; it was shocking. I began to realise that I didn't read by translating the letters into phonetic sounds but I read by recognising each word as an image. I was using words as hieroglyphics. It explained why I struggled so much learning a language with a new alphabet. The whole set of images were so different and my memory couldn't keep up. No wonder the letters were flipped and muddled and cryptic.

There was some discussion about labels. Why have them, why use them, isn't it just boxing you in? *Down with labels*, the world shouts! Sometimes it is pointed out to me that I had done well without knowing, and perhaps if I had known I might have been held back by the knowledge of having a learning difficulty.

I agree that labels can be damaging. I have already talked about how difficult it can be to be labelled as stupid or bad. In an ideal world we wouldn't have any labelling and everyone could live happily without disadvantage and oppression. But we don't live in that world. And, as it stands right now, there can be some real benefits that come with labelling.

Firstly, it helps you to find people going through the same things as you. It's great to have communities to be able to talk about trials and tribulations. You get to celebrate successes with others who might be able to understand what you have gone through to get there. In a similar way they can all rally behind you during tough times and you can talk without having to explain your situation. In other words, it makes you feel less alone, and isn't that all we are seeking on a primal level?

Secondly, those labels and communities are the places where we can find out techniques, tips and new ways of existing. People can offer advice: for example, you could ask how people learn new vocabulary and the community can recommend programs, types of pens, paper, teachers and magical meditations to fix it all (not really). Of course, not everything will work for you. But if you can find one little thing to make life a little easier, in my opinion, it is worth it.

Thirdly, those labels are the things that point out that you are at a disadvantage. With an official diagnosis comes help. Or it should, anyway. We generally accept that learning difficulties are a disadvantage in certain situations. School and work, let's say. So with the label comes extra time in exams, computers, one-to-one mentoring. These are given to try to even out the chasm between those people who can do certain things well and those of us who can't. It can provide people with the time and the tools to be able to show their ability and not purely how well they can write neatly, or construct a grammatically sound sentence. It is crucial for helping individuals show what they are good at without the unnecessary weight of how a *normal brain works*.

Label round my neck, I carried on as normal through my course. My tutors were great, always asking how they could help. My problem was that I hadn't the slightest idea what would help. I had to relearn who I was and how my brain worked. Slowly, I began to piece together little fragments of myself. If I recorded lectures rather than taking notes, I absorbed information better than when in the room, and I could re-listen to make notes rather than leaving the room with illegible untranslatable notes and no grasp of anything the lecturer said. I started to ask tutors to point out which books on a reading list gave an overview of a topic so I could start with that. I needed the big picture before I could look at the specifics of a topic. But usually you would end up with a reading list of twenty-plus books and I was used to just reading what I could find in my closest library.

I'm not sure my essays actually got much better. But I began my dissertation early. I wrote it over nine months alongside the rest of my work. It felt like nothing else I had ever done before. I realised that I could look at how academics wrote, their sentence structure and vocabulary, and copy it but adjusting it with my own argument. Obviously I wasn't literally just nicking it but I mimicked the language and the formats so that I wasn't just sat there wondering how to translate my thoughts onto a blank page. Before, I didn't understand how to write in an academic way, I just plonked things on a page. Here, I realised I could pick out the hallmarks from other texts and manipulate my ideas into their words.

The time and the research was joyful. I used my one-to-one support to get her to show me how to structure and point out where things didn't follow. In the end, I came up with something that, when I reread it, I was astounded that I had written. I explored how euphemism was used in modern art in the depiction of rape in the myth of Leda and the Swan. I looked at how far titillation present in Dali's painting was part of the 'ancient tradition' and whether the explicit violence in Cy Twombly's work could be mirrored in classical depictions. I felt clever and capable of original academic thought! A novelty.

LEDA ATOMICA

DALI
(1949)

CY TWOMBLY
(1962)

I had been exploring various creative things alongside my studies. I had worked on a film magazine, I set up a self-published zine for my college and I was in various stage productions. I did stand-up for the first time (to impress a boy) and it changed my life. Never before had I ever been so scared; I spent a week feeling like I was about to vomit. I did my set over and over again on Skype to my parents. *Why aren't you laughing?* I cried after the twelfth time.

It's only because we've seen it before, said Dad.

You know you don't actually have to do it if you don't want to, said Mum.

But as we got closer to the night, I calmed. The thought of doing it was a thousand times worse than actually doing it. My fear comes with the thought, the idea. It fills me with shame and self-loathing. *Why on earth do you think you can do that, you piece of shit?* But once I've decided I'm doing it, that voice luckily shuts up. Once I've done the planning, I know that I'll get up and do it. That voice is useless; it knows I won't be stopped.

My first set, like most comedians', was the best. People laughed a lot. But, more importantly, I realised that I had created it all. I had written it, it was my story and my persona. I hadn't had to audition or get permission from someone else to make it. That was the revelation for me. It tied up all the things I loved – writing, stories, talking and acting the fool. It became the basis of what I wanted to do. As I moved forward, I was driven to make things where I wasn't limited by the vision of posh kids who had been doing this since school, or who had been seeing plays at the National since infancy (it's a big theatre in London, apparently for the people, but I didn't know what it was until I was twenty-two). I realised that I was more drawn to creating my own path rather than trying to force myself into the ones that existed and weren't particularly interested in me.

Unfortunately, I did have to force myself into my final exams. They were not only unavoidable but also made up almost the entirety of my final results. Oxford is not into coursework or cumulative examining, which is a real shame because the exam system has been proven to benefit specific groups of people (cough, cough white, privately educated men). But I had to sit them even if I knew it was ludicrous and unfair.

At the beginning of my exam term, I got very ill. I had just broken up with Martha and started a new relationship with someone else, so it felt like karma for being a fickle lesbian. It started with horrible tonsillitis (the doctor said *it's the worst I've seen in five years*, which made me feel a bit better as I croakily quoted him to anyone who would listen). Then, after eventually finding the right antibiotics, I got a bit better. But once I could swallow, I started to find lumps all over my body. Lumps are exactly the last thing you ever want to find because we all know what our mind jumps to. I was assured that my inflated lymph nodes were nothing to worry about but the knock-on effect from my infection. But over the following six weeks I got worse. My symptoms seemed to be premature ageing; all my joints seized up and I moved like I was under three tons of water. It turned out I had a thing called erythema nodosum, which was either an early sign of cancer or just a repercussion of the tonsillitis. I had my lungs checked and had scans. I was fine. But there was a period of time where I had to think about dying.

I swung drastically between two extremes (as is my style). Sometimes I was filled with worried panic. I had never been properly ill before. Certainly, no worse than a two-day bug, and this seemed so big and all-consuming that it seemed like the only logical (read: drama queen) conclusion that this would result in my untimely demise. It was the first time that I had to recalibrate my life. I slowed down, I slept for hours and I needed help from other people in a way I had never needed before. When I wasn't trembling with my own mortality, I was quietly stoic. OK, not stoic, but I accepted that I had to be happy with how life had turned out. I had loved and been loved.

But luckily for me the test results came back quick enough before I started planning my eulogies. The real effect of being ill was that it physicalised what previously I couldn't do for my mental state. I had to change my behaviour because it had reached a point in which I had no choice. I was forced to be slow and kind and, most importantly of all, forgiving because my body felt like it was eroded away. As I slowly got better I realised that was exactly the attitude I needed to have with my brain. I had to give myself space and not force myself to do work when I was tired or feeling lost. Just because my mental health and my intellectual space was invisible didn't mean that it wasn't prone to exactly the same tiredness, weariness and pain as my bodily form. I prioritised myself.

So I revised, but I avoided the people around me who were working twelve hours straight. I tried to zone out of the general atmosphere of panic and desperation. I knew that those exams were never going to represent me and my abilities at my best. Just like how, for those few months, it would take me five times longer to get up a flight of stairs, I just had to get through the exams like Frank Sinatra (I did it my way).

Then there was the issue of grades. People are ridiculous about results and perhaps they are even more laughable about it in an academic setting like Oxford. There was a hushed echo all around during the exam period *as long as I don't get a 2:2*. In the queue for lunch, in the library and even in the moments before an exam started, you could hear people chanting it to themselves and to others *as long as I don't get a 2:2*. It pissed me off. I had already got a 2:2 for my Mods and it was fine. I was proud of it and it made me furious that slipping one grade was meant to be this shameful, unthinkable possibility. And I can tell you now, the people who really might have got a 2:2 were not the ones with the mantra. No, it's always the ones you know are going to be fine who have to pass on the fear.

On the other side, you got people who were great at exams who went the other way. One girl kept talking about how disappointed she had been in getting a 2:1 in Mods. She kept saying how she didn't want to be mediocre. *I'd rather get a third than a 2:1*, she said. Which is the sort of thing you only say when you think you're better than everyone else. Like that trying your best is what you do when you are average. When I pointed out that I had scraped my 2:2 she shut up because what she was really saying was that she was only interested in getting a first and that actually she thought it would be embarrassing to try and, in her eyes, fail.

So I had to let go of the grades. I would get what I got but, more importantly, I was going to leave with all the knowledge and experience.

By the time the exams came round I had a routine. I would wake up at six and revise in the morning because it felt like returning back to a world I knew. I had to nap in the afternoon and I went to bed early. On exam days, I would listen to a carefully constructed playlist of punk bangers and pumping dance music. I'd eat a banana and have a coffee dressed in subfusc, just like before. But instead of being seated in the grand hall I was ushered into a side room filled with computers for the group of us with special provision.

Before the first exam I had no idea what it was going to be like; yes, I'd used a computer before but not for a set of exams. The first thing I noticed is that we were allowed spell check, which made my innards rejoice. But in a tight second place came the cacophony of angsty typing as the room around me descended into chaotic pitter-patter. The noise drove me into a worried frenzy. For the remainder of the exams I took in earplugs (my one key piece of advice for everyone sitting exams).

But once I got settled into the process I began to realise what a difference having the special considerations made. It was like I had finally been put in the correct weight division in boxing. Yes, I still had to punch my way through the exam but now I had an actual fighting chance. I was amazed that I had time to plan! Time to read through! Time to go to the toilet!

I realised that the exam was testing my ability to write under certain conditions, not purely my ability to race against time. Surprisingly, in some of the exams I even enjoyed myself. I was writing about things I loved and had studied for four years. Of course, some of them were dreadful but I was lucky, the translation exams were passages I vaguely recognised. I left my final exam knowing I had done my best. I had no clue what grade I would get but, as far as possible, I tried to release myself from being tied down to a silly little number on a piece of paper.[2] I knew that the four years at Oxford had changed who I was. I left feeling a little less clever and a lot more confident in myself. The northern accent had softened but I was still rude, loud and kicking my way forward into the world.

2   For those that care (You shouldn't! Don't you get it by now? Grades don't measure a person!), I got a 2:1 overall for my degree.

CHAPTER 8

FEELING

By the end of the exams I had worked out the limits of my academic brain. That suited me fine; I had no plans to continue onto a MA and a PhD. But I also had an experience in my final year of university which showed me the limit of my brain in non-exam-based terms. It is another odd tradition in Oxford that every three years someone puts on a full production of a Greek tragedy in the original language. I desperately wanted to be in a show at the Oxford Playhouse and I knew that this was my best option. I also suspected that it would help me with my degree somewhat. To my great surprise, I was not only cast but given the lead female role as the goddess Athene.

I started learning my lines. I recorded each one and listened to the speeches on repeat. I had weeks. In rehearsals we practised with scripts. The production was inspired by Francis Bacon's paintings and told the story of the avenging ancient spirits coming to seek justice. We sang and screeched out the Greek, experimenting with ways to make the audience understand what we were saying despite the millennia-old sounds mispronounced by us. There would be surtitles – like at a posh opera – but our impossible aim would be that the audience would just *feel* the meaning.

I usually had a reasonably easy time at learning lines. It's easiest if you have written it yourself, but if worst comes to the worst, in English, you need to learn the flow of the conversation. But in this instance, time hurtled forward and none of the sounds would stick in my head. I knew what the English translation meant but I couldn't get through my three huge monologues at the end. It was just a string of meaningless noises to me. I couldn't make it stick.

By the time we reached the dress rehearsal, the male lead and I had the same panicked look. I threw my script aside and plunged in. For about half of my lines, I completely made up the 'Ancient Greek'. By the time I got to the end of it, I was devastated. Sure, I had a badass costume, the air of an immortal, and even my own theme music composed especially for my entrance – but what was the point if I was talking the equivalent of gobbledegook. The director came to find me and I cried my apologies on her. She had watched the run-through without a script – she claimed not to have noticed that I had been, er, *improvising*. We made a plan – we recorded my final trilogy of speeches and piped them over. The director excitedly said it made complete sense, *It's like a dictator infiltrating the minds of his subjects.* I took it. It was better than the pit of despair that had been sitting within me.

The next day, I could feel the other actors in the chorus look at me. I knew they thought they could have learnt it all. Maybe they could have but, alas, I was the one tasked with it. Even without the last speeches I had to blag my way through. But I guess in some ways I think it's more impressive to have big enough balls to get up in front of all the leading academics and over 600 other members of the public for a week and make up all the words. My parents congratulated me on learning all the lines and, when I told them the truth, they cheered. I had to abandon my hopes of being a professional bard with a specialism in ancient lyric. However, it was my first and only dalliance with fame. For months after, people would stop me in the streets in Oxford to ask if I was the goddess from the Greek play. I think they were too busy trying to work out if I was wearing a wig than listening to the close intricacies of Aeschylus' poetry.

At the end of my degree, I realised that I had no plans. Everyone around me had been doing internships over the summers and applying to grad schemes. I couldn't move back to Batley, not because I thought I was too good for it but because my parents had moved to London. My mum had got on to an MA at the Royal College of Art, and the Stones were on the up and up. I couldn't move in with them because they had a one-bedroom cottage in Cockfosters and *even* I don't like my parents that much.

I often wonder how ambitious I am. I'm driven, definitely, but to be ambitious you have to know exactly what you want and then work back, hitting all the stages to reach that goal. After getting into Oxford, I relinquished the idea of goals. I wanted to take up the opportunities that arose, that I could never predict. I was aware that I could miss out on so much by only focusing on what I knew existed in the world.

Luckily for me, the world did offer up a few things I could never have predicted. Firstly, one of my tutors had organised for a French theatre company to come to Oxford and teach for a couple of weeks. She encouraged me to apply and when I researched the Théâtre du Soleil I was completely blown away. I auditioned in front of some striking-looking middle-aged French ladies dressed in black. When I found out I got the place, I had no idea quite how life-changing the fortnight would be.

It was like a new type of education – the sort you hear people talk about in wistful tones. Each day we went to the theatre, a converted swimming pool, and sat in the stalls. Ariane Mnouchkine, the founder and director of the company, sat at the front on a stool,

which she initially apologised for. She was in her late seventies and I couldn't see why her stool would be an issue for us. But throughout the ecole, she spent very little time on her chair. When she momentarily sat on it, it was merely as a resting place so that when she burst through shouting it was more emphatic. She was not someone to be messed with, which is my favourite sort of person.

On the stage, a tape border is lain out to clearly demarcate the playing space. At the back is a golden curtain, and for a scene to begin the curtains must swing open and the players bounce from the opened space. To be on the stage and not performing was a crime. It was marked out to be a sacred and numinous arena.

Fright is your fiancé for the rest of your life, Madame Mnouchkine proclaimed on the first day. The entire time we would be improvising everything we did on stage. No scripts and no lines. I learnt a lot about life in the moment before I stepped on the stage. Behind the curtain, you may not know what you are about to do or in fact you might, and that can be more terrifying. The weight of fear doesn't lift each time you do it; it should be a forever companion. But the cloth will open like hair parting and you are suddenly the face shining forth. It is your duty to tell the story.

Step into the abyss, she shouted.

In those weeks, I become awake to what it is about performing that I love – the surrender. When you find a state of flow and you stop watching yourself on stage, you are lifted into a state of being free from thinking. It is like your brain no longer has control over you, and for much of my life I have been chained to my thinking. But to have just one fleeting moment of release is to no longer feel a need to do and to be clever but instead to live.

My notes from this period are woefully unable to capture the experience. Partly because I wrote them in pencil (a lesson I have learnt the hard way) and more significantly, because I often found myself in a state of awe. I knew I should be writing down everything but I also knew that it was far more important to live in the moment and absorb the experience. I eventually relinquished any attempt to capture the lesson on the page. How on earth does one write down the moment in which you see the performers from the Théâtre du Soleil?

They had brought around five of their core actors. They were astounding. Some were older and full of firecracker action, others were younger and only able to speak French and Farsi, yet there was no barrier made by age or by language. I saw the players come out from the golden curtain then transport us to ships on storms, riots in cities and a sweeping romance. Every action they made was clear and big and precise. Nothing was easy but everything was nourishing. The work they made before our eyes was full of compassion. The characters on stage interacted with us and Ariane. Nothing was better than when the characters on stage misbehaved and she shouted at them. You would wonder where the line was between reality and theatre until you remembered there was a line literally drawn on the stage.

We, the students, took it in turns on the stage in groups and we tried to touch the hem of what we had been shown by the *professionals*. Sometimes we succeeded. My first time on the stage, I knew I had done well as we moved in unison improvising to big sweeping music which pumped me with emotion. But over the following days, when the music was removed and we were required to improvise scenes and speak, I was stuck. We would try to come up with funny little scenes to impress Madame Mnouchkine: old ladies fighting over a sale, a queue for the toilet when everyone had diarrhoea, a man dancing with a dead body. Some were magical but none of the scenes I was in passed her rigorous eye. I tried to be clever and instead was in a rare state of speechlessness. We were shouted off the stage when what we were doing was bad. She yelled instructions, pointing her hands, making massive gestures in order to help the performers on stage but when it was clear we were not on the right path, we would be unceremoniously ejected from the stage. She was not interested in seeing bad theatre.

After one of the many failed attempts, I spoke to Ariane. *I'm trying but I know I'm too stuck in my head.*

You want it too much. But don't cry, it will come, she replied.

It did come. In the final few days of the school, we were dressed in the ornate costuming and intensely precious masks that the Théâtre du Soleil had brought with them. The mask is an ancient tradition found all

over the world. We were introduced to the western tradition of Commedia dell'arte. Some of the other actors excitedly bustled to show their knowledge of the stock characters. There was the mischievous Arlecchino and the miserly Pantelone. But this was the Théâtre du Soleil; they were not just interested in the western tradition and so they brought out the equally incredible half-masks from Bali. The actors came forward and carefully introduced us to the characters. Some were ingenious and adventurous and others sad and romantic. Each mask was to encourage us to take ourselves out of us as the actor and participate in the sacred traditional characters used for centuries. We were taught the importance of craft and precision. To be original you must honour the great things that have been long established, and not just the high art but the work that was made for the people.

With the penasar masks, the top of your face is covered with hand-painted wooden artefacts. The mask has a top lip and teeth so the wearer's own chin and bottom lip are shown and you can speak clearly. We were dressed in layers of carefully folded cloths with the hems cascading down the front. Flowers were tucked around the outside of the masks. We were made beautiful.

When my time came, I was wearing the Balinese half-mask of Deuchedentes, so called by the Théâtre du Soleil because of his two prominent teeth. I'm not sure of the spelling or the original language of this particular mask's name, but I think he'll forgive me. He is sweet, naive and not the cleverest of all the masked characters but I was very fond of him. When other people had worn him, I had liked how he tried his best but rarely succeeded. That seemed like a familiar and fruitful path for me. But now it was my turn I had tried and failed to make two scenes with other performers in different masks and, just as we were all about to be sent off to undress and remove our faces, Deuchedentes began to speak.

He didn't understand the rules: Madame Mnouchkine wanted us to be prepared but also live in the moment, tell the truth but tell a story, to plan but improvise, to give it our all but not try too hard. He was confused and everyone found his confusion very funny, especially the woman on the stool in the front.

She shouted, *More!* and *Give us your eyes!* The more he spoke the more confused Deuchedentes became and the more everyone else seemed to enjoy it. Then, as they laughed, he became even more muddled as he couldn't understand why everyone thought he was doing a scene right now when all he wanted was some help, a bit of clarification on the rules. After some time, Madame Mnouchkine eventually asked *Deuchedentes? Who is the actor wearing your mask?*

To my surprise, he replied *Kaiya* and I realised that I had been doing it, living on stage and it felt like I had been possessed. Neither me nor Deuchedentes knew the rules before, but only by doing it did I learn to live in the contradiction of it all. I left the stage as bright as the curtain hanging behind me.

But as much as I would have loved to run off to Paris and beg to be a protégé of the Théâtre du Soleil, another mysterious thing had happened and I had to let life show me other plans.

During my time at Oxford, I had met a woman called Milja who I thought was incredibly impressive. She was Dutch, which is like French or German but cooler. She was studying for a second degree having already studied at drama school. A short film she had written was shortlisted for an Oscar – honestly, you

DRAMA

don't get more impressive than that. She was the sort of director I love – she hated pretending. Now that might sound a bit ridiculous if you think that acting is just pretending to be someone else. But only shit acting is that. As I had been taught by the Théâtre du Soleil, it is the duty of the actor to live it. Milja thought that too, and she introduced me to her mentor, an old South African guy called Brian Astbury.

Brian Astbury had worked in theatre for a long time, especially in drama schools training people. His book, *Trusting the Actor*, is wonderful. I had attended a workshop he ran during my time at university. Melodramatically, I had decided that I was going to give up performing. Disheartened by rejections and a lack of roles that said anything to me about my life, I wanted to throw in the towel. But I had signed up for a week-long workshop in London. Over the week we did a lot of emotional work. Pushing walls and doing hundreds of sit-ups while reciting monologues. The passages Brian picked were incredible and it was a joy not only to be a participant but to watch the work produced by the others on the course. It might all sound like a ridiculous boot camp, but not only did it remind me why I loved performing but it reconnected me to storytelling.

So, when out of the blue in the summer of my last year at Oxford I received an email from Brian announcing his establishment of his own year-long course, there wasn't much question that I would be there. He started with the line *You're one of the people I wish to teach before I die* and I fell for it hook, line and sinker. I was going to find the money and sign my year away. I didn't even think.

So I found myself in Guildford for a year. No one else who Brian had emailed had taken the bait – some couldn't find the fees and others didn't want to move their life even temporarily to city suburbia.

The people on my course ended up being an odd set. There were only ten of us at the start of the year. Brian had collaborated with a small man who ran local am-dram classes and together they had pulled together an elite squad. Most of the people who had signed up had originally signed up to be on a TV and film acting course. So there was definitely a bit of a disparity between those of us who wanted to make shows and those who wanted to be famous. Half of the group were eighteen-year-old girls straight from school. There was a musical theatre man and two middle-aged Portuguese actors who drove in every day from London.

The Forge was a one-year course where we would make an entirely new piece of work every five weeks. Each project was headed up by a professional director. It was an answer to the problem of being an actor where you have to wait for someone else to cast you in a piece of work. That was never my fate, I was already making my own work, but I was excited to expand my experience and really invest in my skills as a creator. The course was incredibly designed and the staff were very talented individuals.

I made a lot of work that year. We devised a show set on a tube where I got to play Anne Frank who had survived the Holocaust and, now homeless, lived on the Bakerloo Line. We made an educational show about the historical figures from Guildford. We made a movement piece which was supposed to be set in a psychiatric ward (very GSCE drama) but instead involved more rolling around on the floor than is ever necessary (sorry to the pals in the audience, but it was *art*). I wrote a musical and got a couple of short films under my belt.

It was enlightening to enter a new type of learning, one that was very practical. It forced me out of my head, and my body appreciated that I no longer spent hours crouched over a desk. It was a very different education and for that I am grateful.

During this time, I started to go out properly. I guess maybe some people would call it raving. Most weekends I found myself in a dark sweaty room listening to a DJ. I took the embodied practise I was taught for performing and applied it to dancing for six hours to house, techno, disco. Sure, the drugs helped, but it was transformational. Dancing gave me a relationship to my body that I had never had before. It erased the years of tripping and torturous PE lessons. My mortal cage became a space in which I was welcome. I learnt how to be in myself alone and how to have a collective shared moment with those around me. It's the closest I have ever felt to touching the hem of spirituality.

But in spite of all that, I was not very happy at all that year. I had moved to a town alone. My nearest supermarket was a petrol station, and I only had one electric hob in the room I was staying in. So I ate depressing food and was incredibly lonely. I don't say this easily, but Guildford is far far worse than Batley. It feels like someone who has never had any fun designed it. The shops are mainly overpriced middle-class status-symbol brands – Le Creuset and Jo Malone. It was a shock to the system. At weekends, I would either return to Oxford to see my partner and go dancing or I would visit my parents in London. I cried on the train back to Guildford every single Sunday. It felt like something I had to survive because I knew it was integral to expanding my skill set and becoming a better storyteller.

I guess if I was producing work that I thought was excellent it might have lessened the blow, but I know that suffering doesn't automatically lead to great art. It just makes you feel shit.

While the course itself was excellently designed and implemented, there were institutional problems – some things can be forgiven and attributed to the premiere of a brand-new thing. However, there are problems that I believe occur in most educational and arts organisations. Although this school tried to be innovative in its course, it failed to question the hierarchical systems that schools engage in. It also failed to question some other old-school ideals and so I will do the questioning here...

The tough love attitude has stuck around far longer

than it needs to. There is something to be said for the obligation of care necessary in all institutions, regardless of the age of the participants. Treating adults with kindness, respect and compassion must be an explicit aim in workplaces, educational systems and in political organisations. For some reason, we seem to think that the moment we're dealing with adults that the basic tenets of human decency can fly out the window in preparation for the so-called *real world*. I am passionately against the concept that people can treat you harshly, rudely and cruelly with the idea that if you can't handle it now you won't be able to flourish *out there*. You are not teaching someone a lesson to toughen up. You are enacting that violence. It is merely the first step to saying that it is acceptable behaviour. You are the instigator of an abuse of power. This is something I have encountered time and time again in almost all institutions I have been a part of. Sometimes it is related to not receiving proper help in terms of my SpLDs and sometimes it is a failure to address power imbalance. However, I had hoped that a pioneering new institution would have been a little more original.

I don't necessarily disagree with the idea of hard work; in fact I pride myself on hard work. But the problem comes when we are forced to feel like our value is linked to our productivity. That if we don't fill every hour with self-improvement, with exercise or practise then we are worthless shits who are bound to fail. It just doesn't sit well with me. It, like most things, is a paradox. Hard work and perseverance is linked to success (though certainly doesn't guarantee it) but also overworking and obsession leads to sickness. It makes you unhappy, tired and burnt-out. My pet hate is being told to work harder and later, perhaps because I already know my limits, having crossed them many times.

The most frustrating thing, however, is to have people in positions of power – usually teachers or mentor figures or bosses – espouse this attitude of working yourself to the bone. The people who listen and consume the message are often the ones already trying their best and it becomes part of an internalised system of self-flagellation. I hate the message of never-ending, ever-increasing hard work. It is disingenuous and it is weaponised. We need to be taught and guided into a healthy attitude to work. Otherwise, we become single-minded, success-at-any-cost individuals with mental health problems and poor personal relationships. We see our success as something that comes with a cost. You shove people under the bus, you blame and you betray. It sends out the message that this is a cut-throat world where there isn't enough for everyone. So I say, down with the doomed genius figure! Viva la early bedtime, good meals and fun with friends alongside accomplishing what you need to!

The other thing that I wish would be eradicated from schools, workplaces and the arts in general is a pervasive lack of encouragement. Who doesn't love a bit of positive affirmation? It is hard to carry on when you receive very little. In Guildford we worked hard and pushed and pushed. It felt at times like being in one of those families where nothing is good enough. My parents are very honest, they'll tell me if they enjoyed work and give me pointers, but alongside that is encouragement. Even if it's a *well done for surviving that*. But the course maintained the attitude that if you're looking for confirmation, then look elsewhere.

There will always be times when you feel like dog shit under someone's shoe. There are days when you don't want or can't get out of bed because you think even your breathing is wrong. *I'm taking up valuable oxygen*, you might whisper into bed sheets you should have changed weeks ago. We do have to learn to find the strength internally to keep going and ignore those voices. You must be the one to pull yourself out of that muddiness. But it is important to remember that the voices in your head that are horrid and cruel come from plonkers who in the past tried to make you feel bad in a misguided attempt to try to make themselves feel better (or because they think they're doing you a favour). But one of the key tools for fighting those voices is to have an armoury of examples that prove them wrong. Each tiny victory is evidence of your success. I know I can't be alone in taking a lot of strength from the people who champion me. Their voices and their comments make it bearable to do the difficult work, to get up and make the work.

However, there was one very notable piece of positive affirmation I received on the course at Guildford. Towards the end of the year we were introduced to our film tutor, Mark. He was brash and loud. Sitting us down he clearly laid out what he expected from us. Strictness is not a part of tough love, it is in fact clear communication. Necessary both for boundaries and also important to waiver when situations call for it. Mark was very definite on the behaviour he demanded from us and treated us like adults. However, he was gobby and northern and in charge. I found him infuriating, mainly because he was inhabiting the role I liked to play.

On the last day of working with him, Mark sat me down and gave me my feedback for the module. He spent a solid amount of time with me and he outlined my strengths and weaknesses. To this day, he gave me the best career advice I have ever received. He told me that I could achieve whatever I set my heart to but that I had to decide what that was. It is something I come back to a lot. Also I like to imagine the words *truly exceptional talent* were uttered, but I have the sneaking suspicion that might be delusional thinking on my part.

The other thing Mark pointed out was that he recognised a lot of himself in my behaviour. An obsessive focus, loudmouth tendencies and easily distracted by noisy or busy environments. Nobody had ever really looked at me like that before. He leant in and said, *I have ADHD. Do you think maybe we're similar in that way too?*

Laughing, I pushed that comment aside. I focused on the rest of what he said. But at the end of the year we were given space to make our own work separate from the group if we wanted. I started on a performance project that I had been researching and thinking deeply about for many years: *Everything is Going to be K.O.*

I knew I couldn't be the only one in this position. There had to be millions of us adults only just finding out about being neurodivergent. But when I looked for stories and books or videos, all I seemed to find was information for parents with young children. So I did what I do best, which is start to tell my own story.

For five weeks I worked on an early version of this project, which took the form of a solo-theatre piece. I wrote thousands of words. I got lost in notes and reading and the emotions that come with rooting through your past.

One particular day, I was in the dark depths of the creative process. A space I like to call initial self-doubt. I was trying to turn crooked notes into neat funny text that someone somewhere might think was clever. But at the same time I was also on the Internet. I had twenty-five tabs open, including a YouTube video and music playing simultaneously. The room I was working in was noisy: it was, after all, the backroom of a pub. I kept starting new sentences and new documents and following new thought threads. Each time a new revelation occurred I would jump down that path for a few moments until another idea showed itself. I was tying myself up.

For one second, I seemed able to lift myself out of this knot just long enough to look at where I was and my behaviour. It terrified me.

I was desperately looking for something interesting enough to quiet the noise in my brain just for a second. The foraging was not working. Instead the manic rummaging just created chaos, both in my brain and my computer screen. Yet all the over-stimulation left me in a state of complete apathy. On that day, I thought back to what Mark had said and with great regret accepted that perhaps, maybe, he could be right.

Like with all new revelations, I threw myself into research. I was shocked to learn how few women and girls were diagnosed with ADHD (and the gap between white kids and everyone else is also horrifying, as with all other diagnoses of SpLDs). Because we have been taught to be nice quiet little girls, often ADHD can manifest itself slightly differently – not as the typical jumping about and hyperactivity but more day-dreaming and insularity.

I find it very hard to contain the thoughts in my head and I tend to blurt out when I'm speaking. I try my best not to interrupt and I think I've got better at it, but before this day in Guildford I hadn't really thought about why I did that. It wasn't that I thought what I was saying was the most important and needed to be heard. In fact, it is a bit like thinking is not even being done by my brain. Thoughts seem to tumble out of my mouth and that is how I know that it was even mulling within me.

But things began to sieve themselves out when I discovered the emotional side of this ADHD. I have always been quite intense. Perhaps it is just my personality. But my highs are high. They soar full of love and generosity, seeing ribbons of light and liquid stars. Kinship vibrates in me when I'm good. Interconnectivity is suddenly easy and apparent. Your joy is mine, my success is shared and bountiful. I hand my heart out to strangers. I always have. Like I said before, I'm a romantic.

But of course, when I'm bad, I am raging. I bubble and spit and scream. I see blackness and furies haunt me. What is most terrifying is that these feelings are tidal. They aren't states I visit. They are possessive. They often feel like they own me. I think that's what people on the outside struggle most to understand about me. I can hit the roof, my hair aflame, and in less than half a minute the feeling will have fallen from my hand like a snotty tissue. I'm very transparent. What you see is very much what you get.

But when I began to read about ADHD and the heightened emotional episodes which can characterise it, I laughed. Those intense highs and lows, the single-mindedness and compulsive behaviour certainly looked familiar. Well, I thought, *Dyslexia, dyspraxia and ADHD – things certainly sound better in threes.*

This is the point in which I should talk about self-diagnosis. Now, it gets a bad rap. There is a tendency for scaremongering, papers quiver with indignation about over-diagnosis and fake conditions. I'm sure that this might be more of a problem with parents and children. In some ways it is understandable, it is tied to a worrying medicalisation that seems to sweep us. We want things to pin our problems on, medication to take the edge off. I've seen the righteous documentaries with young kids pilled up and erratic because parents can't control little Timmy, when really he's just dying for a bit of attention and a laugh.

But really, the majority of people that I know who are self-diagnosed are adults who for the first time, via the Internet, find the information about what SpLDs are. It is worth noting that, obviously, a professional diagnosis would be preferred. We would all love the official stamp and the recognition that comes with it. But it is not a low-cost exercise; an assessment with an educational psychologist is going to cost you over £700. I don't have that sort of money and neither does large swathes of the population. So it then becomes a question of what you want and need the official tag for. Because I already have my official bit of paper saying that I'm dyslexic and dyspraxic, I am protected by the law and can demand institutional support. You need the bit of paper to get the extra time, for example. For certain things you can get an assessment through the NHS, but the waiting lists are long.

For many people, self-diagnosis is the first step at looking at themselves and their lives. Is it making them happy? How do they relate to the world around them? It enables there to be some self-reflection and a framework in which to understand their childhood and adult experiences. No one should be made to feel shit for wanting to understand what is going on within them. It is admirable and brave. Much like my earlier discussion on labels, self-diagnosis is an important stage for individuals seeking support from communities, to look for encouragement and help. It is also important to remember that a large part of an assessment involves anecdotal exploration: a professional will ask: Did you learn to read late? Do you feel alone? How do you experience time? It's not a blood test. You can ask yourself those same questions.

By doing that, I have found it very useful to look at my behaviour and take steps to make small changes. I would love to get an official diagnosis but there are obstacles in the way. I'm not sure I see the point. I still don't know how I feel about ADHD medication. My personal and recreational studies in uppers (i.e. drugs that don't make you sad) have found them astoundingly effective at creating mental clarity. But I am unsure about whether I want that focus every day. I have harnessed my obsession and hyper focus and chaos. I have managed to move my life around how I operate. It is easier for me to mould the city, the day, the work around me than to disassemble my engine room and rewire my brain.

I also, ironically, am so scattergun in organising my life that I haven't been registered at a GP's for four years. When I finally rectify that, after six months of having the phone number on a tab lost among seventy-eight other apparently essential web pages, how on earth am I supposed to suddenly whip out the organisational skills to make myself an appointment? I can't help but feel that, if I could do it easily, I wouldn't lose my keys and phone and I wouldn't need to be put on a waiting list for non-brand Adderall...

CHAPTER 9

WORKING

There was no other type of school that I wanted to spend any more time in after the Forge. So I assumed that the world of work was waiting for me. I was ready to get my career started – as what, I wasn't entirely sure. But I needed to start climbing the greasy pole, to get my name on the map. The world wouldn't know what had hit it.

I had high hopes for myself in the sense that I aspired to be able to do exactly what I wanted all day every day and be paid for it. Alas, it didn't take me long to come crashing down to earth and discover that the world wasn't remotely interested in funding my idle lifestyle as a modern dandy. I had to forge my own path and make my own future.

Firstly, I had to find somewhere to live in London. It would be a cliché to talk about how that is an impossible task, and so all I will say is that searching for a habitable, affordable, commutable nest became my first full-time job. I spent hours on websites and the number of tabs grew and my poor laptop whirred like it was about to take off. My brain felt the same as I tried to remember exactly where the tubes ran and how much council tax might be and what sort of fees I'd have to pay and to who. My weekday consisted of viewings and inane conversations with letting agents who would call me at 9 a.m. each morning. *How was yesterday for you?* they'd ask. I'd have to rack my brains to work out if I had inadvertently ended up on a date while looking round a tiny new-build with a single cupboard of storage for four adult inhabitants. I looked at over twenty properties until I accepted that I would have to pay twice what I expected on rent or live in a damp subterranean hovel. I let Charles Christmas, the letting agent, down lightly (yes, real name *and* his birthday was 25 December – I saw his driving licence).

Aged twenty-three, I had become thoroughly institutionalised. Nothing really prepared me to have all that comes with being in a school or university suddenly removed. I was excited for my new-found freedom but I was not prepared for the responsibility. I now began to realise that I hadn't been taught much in terms of practical skills. Luckily, I had managed to gain confidence with cooking, but that was essentially the extent of my adult competence. Sneakily, in university I managed to find the world's greatest housemate, Nick, and I haven't let him go since. He took care of sorting out bills and so even to this day that part of my life administration is luckily taken care of. But, unfortunately, I could not subcontract the business of job hunting.

It was at this point in my life when I realised that I was truly awful at writing applications. I was looking for a job and I really only had my heart set on something in the arts. I wasn't too picky. Initially, I looked at admin jobs and the first one I applied for gave me a really encouraging response. Heartened, I ploughed on. But after months of not only rejections but mainly radio silence I began to wonder what on earth companies wanted. Apparently, I had a degree from a prestigious institution and I was extremely keen. Entry level job rejections I could handle, but I was also getting ignored for bar work and front-of-house roles in theatres.

One of the greatest problems of applying for jobs in this modern era is the invention of the application portal. Firstly, they make you start accounts as if you'll be logging back in to apply for more jobs from them. Trust me, after trying to wrangle with the web page for a couple of hours, wild horses wouldn't drag me back.

Secondly, I have never managed to find a way of looking at the entirety of an application. If you can't see all the questions/activities, it is basically impossible to structure your answers and decide what information goes where. Sometimes they don't give you full details of the job until AFTER you have uploaded your cover letter, automatically meaning that your cover letter isn't tailored to the role.

All of these things are a problem for everyone but more than that, they are extremely unhelpful for people who, like me, have SpLDs. The time it takes for me to fill in each individual box asking all sorts of silly questions that could be answered by my CV is multiplied by about seven because I have to draft and redraft each answer. Plus, let's not even talk about the fact that these forms in browsers seem to facilitate spelling and formatting errors. It adds an additional barrier to job opportunities. Each time I see that a job or scheme requires a portal application I know that I will have to sink at least a week into trying to get my head around both the website and the language to express myself.

Thankfully, there are some schemes which if you declare a disability and you have the required qualifications you automatically get an interview. For a while, I dithered. Surely, I wasn't disabled enough. But after another few rejections I had to accept that I was failing to represent myself accurately. I looked up the definition of disability under the 2010 Equality Act. To qualify you must *have a physical or mental impairment that has a 'substantial' and 'long-term' negative effect on your ability to do normal daily activities.* I decided that if I got extra time and help legally given to me at university then that must mean that the effect of my SpLDs clearly melded into my daily life. I recalibrated my attitude to the word disabled. Instead of just thinking about physical impairments, I expanded my understanding. People with serious mental health issues clearly are impacted; the sensory overload from autism and speech impairments can all restrict daily life.

By looking outward at the experiences of others and how they deserved additional support and protection in the workplace, I was able to turn and reflect on myself. Why was I hesitant to tick the box that said disabled? I thought I didn't need the help (I'm stronger than that), or that receiving the help would make people think that I was stupid and lazy and a cheat. All of those thoughts came from internalised ableism (discrimination against disabled people). I was full of contradictions. I thought I shouldn't tick the box because then people would see how long it took me to write or they'd see how tied up I could get in words and they'd think I was useless. But I also thought I shouldn't tick the box because I believe that I am talented, clever and able – which by proxy means that I thought being disabled stopped you from being any of those things. That is fucked up. Being disabled doesn't automatically rule you out of being an excellent, high-achieving human being but somewhere inside me I thought that was the case. So I had to start consciously unbelieving those pernicious, self-hating thoughts. I also accepted that to be the best I could be, just like in university, that I would take all the help I could get.

On the Internet, I found an abundance of disabled and neurodiverse voices. Their successes and difficulties shone a light on so many things. They taught me a great deal about the ways in which language enforces those shitty beliefs. With them I got enraged about how society will laud disabled people as inspiring and still refuse to put in place the correct accommodations to enable us to shine. After all this I reflected on the term disabled and how society's reluctance to use it implied that it was something to be ashamed of. Each time someone mentions special needs or differently abled I began to see that they couldn't accept that disabled was in fact a neutral term. There isn't anything inherently bad about disability; the limiting factors are not in the person but rather the world around us. The classic example is that a wheelchair is not the thing that limits its user, in fact it is the very thing that gives them freedom. Stairs and small doorways and prejudice are the constraints. The world needs to become more accessible. I realised that to ensure that I made the world fairer, I needed to ask for the provisions I needed and I proudly had to become a member of a broad community that I am honoured to participate in. So I started ticking the box.

Once I had made that decision, it was easier for me to get my head around the situation. But I began having these conversations a lot with my family. At my own diagnosis, my mum had done her own research, proclaiming that surely all of the telltale signs of dyslexia were normal, it was how she experienced things. We realised that it was hereditary. The hours that we spent working in the Stone household started to look a little different, less like raw ambition and a little more like extreme coping mechanisms. My parents were always so proud of my and Cas's academic achievements, especially in the light of their own seeming lack of schooling. But, instead, now we can see that this wasn't some freak accident. No, they had slipped through the gaps, hadn't received the proper help. It would explain why Mum hadn't done as well in her O-levels as she had in her mocks. The following summer after I had been diagnosed, Cas went for an assessment and joined me in the dyslexia and dyspraxia double. When Mum went to do her MA, she had to accept that it was taking her hours to produce her written work. She read and read, wrote and redrafted. She worked constantly but she was hesitant to go and get a diagnosis despite my pushing. I understood. She relented and got an assessment. She joined the dyslexia gang. No surprises there.

But there was another turn of events. I was looking into why women and girls are vastly underdiagnosed with SpLDs and how certain behaviours (noisy, disruptive and 'naughty'), which can flag it up, are found mainly in boys. Whereas, girls can be quieter and subdued if struggling or uninterested in school so are likely to be overlooked. Also, because women and young girls are raised to be nice and thoughtful and selfless, they might try to hide any difficulties. I became fascinated by how diagnostic criteria seemed to be skewed towards the behaviours of men and boys. I looked at so-called female traits of autism (which just means more subtle and often better-masked attributes) and was struck by it. It sounded a lot like my younger brother. These so-called *masculine* and *feminine* trait concepts let down everyone, irrelevant of gender.

I kept replaying a fraught conversation we had when he was a teenager. Casius felt so disconnected from the world, he felt everything more than everyone else, it was all so intense. I dismissed him; we all feel like that, I always feel like that. I felt dreadful and so guilty. I wasn't listening but I guess we also didn't know what to listen out for. So when I read something that sounds familiar, I sent him an article and after a long waiting list, he was diagnosed as being on the autistic spectrum. It may be late; I know that feeling well. The anger at how on earth one can slip through the gaps. Understandably, he is struck with the frustration and the pain. *Why didn't you know? How did I survive all this time without knowing? You should have had me tested.* But when my dad read Cas's report, he was hit by the familiarity of experience. My parents could never have known because nobody tested them, and if they never had the context to realise their own neurodivergence how on earth could they recognise it in us? What we see is that they worked around it, created a new path and flourished. But now they can take the new revelations and adjust to make things a little easier. It is never too late to learn to transform and accept new complex parts of ourselves.

The new complex part of myself that I had to hone was patience and an ability to mop up vomit from a urinal. Because, when I eventually got a job, it was in a bar. The manager had asked me in to interview because my CV was in colour and had a logo on it. I worked on Battersea Rise for a year and a half. During Oxford I had worked in my college bar (remember pound a pint?). It was a very lax, student-run job but I had enjoyed both the busyness and the extra cash. Moving over to a proper professional bar I was worried about a whole list of things, in particular how many glasses I would inevitably smash. I'd like to say it was an unnecessary worry but I did create a trail of shattering glass. But I soon realised that the majority of service work is cleaning, so a few more broken pint glasses weren't a big deal.

The first couple of months my body was on fire. I was pretty fit; I had been going to the gym and was accustomed to long hours. But my legs and feet and back kept seizing up after the hours of standing. I would finish a shift and head home only to lie awake pumped with adrenaline. My morning-person status soon disappeared as I started to see a lot more of what happens in the early hours of a weeknight. I met a lot of foxes and crossed many a road to avoid meeting men on the pavement. I had found my workplace a mere five-minute walk from my new flat and on particularly cold nights or occasions when I was struck by fear (of being followed... or a car veering off the road... or an escaped wild dog, or...) I would run the journey home.

Bar work gave me two wonderful things. Firstly, it gave me the joy of doing. I had spent so long sitting, reading and thinking. My back was curved over from years of concaving over a desk. Apart from the crooked neck, the worst thing about that is that you become cerebral – stuck in the prison of your own mind. Bar work requires thinking, don't get me wrong. You have to be focused and quick and charming, but most importantly of all it requires action. It doesn't matter how hard you try, you cannot think your way out of a pile of washing-up or a puddle of unidentified slush in the gents.

Secondly, it showed me the benefits of proper teamwork. Perhaps because I'm not a team-sports kind of person and perhaps because those sorts of activities are still embedded with competitive violent energy, I had never really got the working with other people thing. I'd always wanted to! In theatre, there is collaboration but a bit like with sports, someone always wants to be the best or wants the credit. I was blessed with an awesome group of people in my bar team. It eroded my natural misanthropic tendencies. People would cover your shift at the drop of a hat and on busy nights when we were in a state of chaos we would stay extra hours, squeezing behind the bar to alleviate the pressure. We gossiped about regulars and drank many late-night pints. It was a bond forged by hard work.

Moving to London initially did weird things to me. I had been looking forward to it for years but, perhaps as an aftershock of Guildford, I found myself fraying a little around the edges. I had never been an overly fearful person unless of course you count the tongue-holding and the late nights of collaging all my failures into one music video of piteous calamity. Often instead of worrying too much about mentally calculating exits, suspicious figures and hazards, I would mentally settle on accepting a quick death. But in London I became certain that I would die tragically in an accident. (Wait, again? Really must bring this up with my therapist.) My logical brain tried to persuade me to let go, to remind me that most people in the world are completely unconcerned with me and have their own important lives to worry about without troubling themselves with me.

It felt like I was falling. I didn't know what to do. I desperately wanted some sort of security (financial, creative, job, personal). The bar work was meant to be a bridge job, something to see me through until I got started, on what I'm not sure. A sort of rebound relationship after university and before the big sweeping romance of my career. But I realised that the getting started was a false idea. I was alive, wasn't I?

Life was happening, there was nothing to stop it from pushing onwards like a wormhole. Even though I could feel the wind rushing in my hair as I plummeted into the future, I felt stagnant. My goals and ambitions crossed their arms and looked disappointedly at my inability to satisfy them. Nobody was saying this to me. It was self-inflicted.

I managed to get some support from the Old Vic for initial development of the show version of *Everything is Going to be K.O.* They gave me a week's rehearsal space. I commuted to Bermondsey each weekday. In the room, I couldn't string a sentence together; I lay down and cried. The walls were thin so I kept down my sobs. I wish I could say as much for my neighbours, whose every single word floated its way into my space. My brain was overwhelmed by my own inability to emotionally regulate and next door's conversations about blowjobs. I was sad and muddled and a little bit titillated.

I watched on as other Oxford graduates around me got to live in their London family homes. I was spending well over half of my pay check on rent and desperately saving money to fund my creative ambitions. Somehow, even the other people who were creatively ambitious and didn't have *proper jobs* seemed to be able to afford to go on holiday. All my money went on rent, saving and pints. There was nothing to spare. It took me a good eight months before I realised that they must be getting money from their parents. I tried not to be furious (I would have done the same if it was an option) and focused on being furiously hard-working instead. I thought I had to be so good that the industry couldn't ignore me.

I managed to get some highly sought-after unpaid work with some film companies. In the year 2017, I worked two jobs. I interned with three of the biggest film companies in the  UK and was not paid for a single hour of my work. Each day I would go and work in an office for at least seven hours and then run off to the bar to get paid (thankfully) the London living wage for a night shift. I loved the excitement of the work I did with the film companies. Powered on by the idea that at the end of it all I would get a paid job in this illustrious industry, I pushed through. That is not to say I didn't complain to all my friends and family. I am not even remotely stoic.

I was hanging on in the hope that I would eventually be given the stamp of approval from an illustrious institution. It had worked for Oxford. I single-mindedly ploughed that path until they let me in. I thought this industry might be the same. I'm a good runner (the first job you get on a film set, not the athletic kind). I'm a stickler for being on time and I guess the novelty hadn't worn off so I was still smiling when dashing about collecting dry-cleaning and buying people's Christmas presents. I wanted the monthly pay check and the foot in the door.

I came very close to getting the very thing I wanted. I got to the last two for the role of assistant to an illustrious film and theatre director. It was my dream entry-level job (if such a glamorous thing can exist). His career straddled the two industries I loved. He wasn't straight, so I could put aside any fears of getting felt up (I had a brief stint at the Weinstein Company; I harbour no illusions of workplace safety). I knew the other candidate and I was confident that I was the best person for the role. The people who were deciding thought differently.

We think it's a waste of your creative talent, they said, which is the opposite of a backhanded compliment. *You'll be bored here. You won't have time to make your own work.* I was utterly heartbroken. I had been struggling to make ends meet both financially and emotionally. I had been burning the candle at both ends with this very objective in mind. I had fallen into the familiar art of working obsessively in order to achieve a competitive goal. But here I was, sat in the cafe of the Old Vic crying because two industry bulwarks wanted me to make my own work instead of chasing after a Hollywood film director. With hindsight, I can accept that this was an incredible endorsement. But those words at the time were hard to swallow. I was exhausted and poor. They felt so far away from where I was in that moment. I didn't know where on earth I was going to get the money to make my own work or to see the theatre they suggested to me. More importantly, I didn't have the energy; I had been pouring it into trying to get an entry-level job.

I realised that they were saying what a lot of people in the industry had been saying to me the whole time. *Make your own work. You'll get stuck in the office or in a role you don't care about if you pursue it this way.* I'm not sure if I agree with them. I wanted to be in that world where people get to make big ambitious projects. It is important to see other people do it. Otherwise, it is a big abstract goal that seems unachievable.

However, it was settled, not by my own hand. I would have to do it the hard way. (There is no easy way nor is there one direct path to what I want to do.) I would have to plough on with my own projects. I resolved to stop working for free for companies that wouldn't give me a job and I decided that I would try to find a new source of income that wasn't bar work.

I had been tutoring one student for a couple of years and my hourly rate was considerably higher than what I was getting in the bar. Harbouring the illusion that I was just weeks away from a full-time job, I resisted taking on any more students. After I realised nobody was going to end my financial woes, I jumped fully into tutoring.

Now I'm a private tutor, which basically means I go to people's homes and give their kids a hand. Sometimes that's with homework, largely it is for upcoming exams. But the jobs I like best are long-term placements because the work is more varied. It could be focused on helping a child explore their creative writing or helping a teenager with her conversational English because it's her fourth language.

It is not wasted on me that I am now partly a teacher. I have become the very thing I swore I wouldn't. Well, I guess I had the full range of experiences and I can try to offer the things that helped me. It is somewhat cruel that I have landed myself in a position where I am still kept awake the night before results day.

I love my job. I get to go into people's homes and nose around their lives. (Taps that make boiling water! Ice machines! Wait, is that an original oil painting?) I get to play a significant role in the lives of several teenagers, usually at a point in their lives when they don't have (m)any personal relationships with adults who aren't related to them. I'm close enough in age to them to show them some sort of future but still old enough to be some form of authority figure.

Academically, I tend to fill in the holes in their learning from school: I make sure kids have covered their whole syllabuses, that they know what the exam will look like and how to tick the boxes required by a mark scheme. A lot of the time, it's the sort of teaching and work that I hated as a kid. It was the stuff I had no idea how to do. Perhaps that is why I like it now. It feels a bit like rewriting the past. I'm giving these kids what I needed.

I almost entirely teach kids with at least one form of SpLD. It's not a coincidence. When I sit with them each week and pour the attention on them and show them the small specificities required by the exams, I am retroactively transforming my school experience. I get to tell them the things I needed to hear. I show them how I passed my GCSE maths exam by writing my times tables in the margins so I didn't have to rely on my poor working memory. I get to read their stories and get excited by the twists and turns. I point out how I love it and how it makes me feel. My ambition is to channel all the teachers who filled me with passion and excitement for learning. At the very least, I want to make it just a little less painful and a little more survivable.

But, really, my job is almost exclusively pastoral care. Sure, I know the contents of the exams and have read the books, etc., but often these kids are the ones who have somehow been left behind. They can't guess or they dare not be wrong. Usually, teachers have singled them out and humiliated them in front of a group. My job is to make them feel safe and to encourage them to think for themselves (and by consequence, pass exams).

How lucky I have been to be given the opportunity

to see the education system from this new angle. I no longer have to sit the exams or even place one foot in a classroom yet I get to try to help kids who have to jump through those hoops. It is a very special relationship. In many ways it feels very sacred, and ironic. I had spent years explaining how our education system fails huge swathes of society and then, suddenly, I'm given the chance to offer some small alternative, to put my money where my mouth is.

I wish I had the words to write a paean for all the wonderful teachers out there who pour themselves into their jobs and never get the credit they deserve. It's a tough job. I would never want to be in their shoes. They do not get paid enough, nor do they get the support they need. Our education system is getting squeezed and squeezed. Its aims are narrow and its targets are a string of numbers. I'm not just talking about our public school system. I can wholeheartedly say the private schools in our country fail their pupils too, just with a bigger bill. Sure, maybe they have water polo, but some of the kids I have taught from illustrious institutions are traumatised and still unable to think critically. Also, because they're private schools, often their SEN (Special Educational Needs) departments can be woefully lacking. I have heard some dreadful tales of kids with SpLDs encouraged to leave because the school won't offer the proper support and they are uninterested in keeping kids who might risk bringing the school's results down.

I always joke that my speciality is difficult teenagers, and that's because I have such an affinity for them. I understand that they're stuck in the in-between world of childhood and adult responsibilities. They want to be hugged, reassured and their dinner to be made for them but at the same time they are pushing to experiment with freedom, bad decisions and their identity outside the family unit. I'm trying to provide them with the safety so they can ask all the questions that keep them up at night, which we've all thought but for some reason think that it singles us out to be the biggest freak in the world. (*When will my period start? Am I gay? Why doesn't anyone like me? Why do my nipples hurt? What's the point in all of this? Am I weird?*)

I homeschool one teenager, so I see him around four days a week. He's a school refuser (which means exactly what it sounds like) and is, honestly, one of my favourite people in the world. There is something humbling about turning up to work each day only for him to look up at me and say, *Eugh, why are you here?* We read books every day but he much prefers when I make up stories for him. We have a long-running tale of a pair of siblings called Boy and Girl. Their parents are pirates but the children just want to go to normal school and have a normal life. I have to make up each episode on the spot. It's hard work to improvise. But we have motifs and phrases that always repeat – which is literally how ancient epic poems – like the *Odyssey* and the *Iliad* – were recited. It is something that he and I share.

Then I go home and write. I've been writing this book in the evenings and my days off from tutoring. Every day is different for me, which is great because it keeps me engaged and fascinated in a way I'm not sure a normal office job would provide. I plan the lessons, but sometimes someone might have a meltdown (not necessarily me) or something completely unexpected arises. We have breakthroughs. Someone understands algebra suddenly or becomes obsessed with space. I get to have moments of intensity and moments of quiet. The part of my life where I sit and type at my desk can be quite isolating. I can spend hours with myself working and reworking my thoughts for this book and other pieces of work, trying to wrangle a drop of an idea out into something more tangible. When I get to leave the house and be silly with my students, it reminds me what is important. Does my work have a good story, is it funny, would the kids get it?

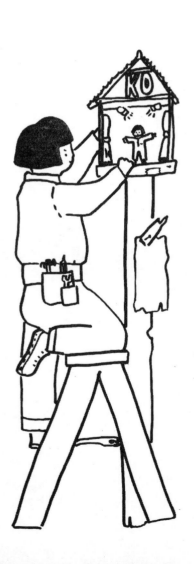

CHAPTER 10

MAKING

The moment that I walked out of that meeting where the word dyslexia was first mentioned, I began to write down everything that happened in relation to this story. I made notes and notes about the assessment, about the things people said offhand about the whole thing. Like a magpie or a hoarder, I tried to pile up all I could about the topic of SpLDs. I would spend hours on the Internet, bookmarking and copying quotes.

I realised that not many people at all were talking about experiences like mine. Despite feeling I was an individual with unique circumstances, I also believed that there must be others out there like me. I was certain there was bound to be so many of us in the same situation. But I couldn't find this group. I joined groups on Facebook and had my notifications inundated with Sharons and Lindas enquiring about *normal handwriting for a boy in Year 3* or *how to get a private diagnosis for their daughter.* Those things are important but I couldn't help think that seeing as SpLDs are hereditary that lots of these mums might also have the same problems as their kids.

I read lots of interesting science books, which gave me some of the language in which to understand the ways in which my brain functions. I turned to crip theory (which is a critical discourse which intersects with queer theory and argues that disability is something to be acknowledged and celebrated) and looked at the politics of disability. I found the most solace and understanding in the writing and work exploring lived experiences of autism by autistic people. I discovered the term neurodiversity – the radically obvious notion that all of our brains work differently, and those different ways mean that our skill sets vary. The key part of this is to note that the world is built to enable one type of brain and any divergence from this supposed 'normal' is seen as defective or worse. That is where we must work to change the world.

It is not enough to simply say people work differently; it is crucial to ask how we can re-evaluate how we value individuals. We all benefit hugely from the exciting lateral thinking of the neurodivergent (those of us with dyslexia, dyspraxia, autism, ADHD and other SpLDs and LDs). We have pioneered new moments in art, science, engineering. We have been entrepreneurs who have thought underneath, around and through problems. We are writers who have taken millions of people on journeys through time and space.

But my reading did not lead me to stories. I wanted to hear about the journeys that people made, from the kids who struggled to learn to read into the adults they became. I wanted to see the array of options for me. But the best I could find were speculative lists of significant figures like Einstein and F. Scott Fitzgerald.

I wanted to hear what it felt like to live in this muddled place, about the joys and difficulties. But the more I looked, the more I realised that rather than spending more time searching, that I should make the thing I needed. Once I got the title, I knew I had no choice but to make the work I was seeking.

It took many years. From the start of the idea to performing at the Edinburgh Fringe, it took me five years. That might sound like an age, but you can't judge – I'm allowed extra time.

I started by writing an awful play which was a thinly veiled autobiography, and after my first draft I knew that it was cowardly to pretend that this wasn't my experience. I also decided that I wanted to get up and perform my own story. I wanted to stand up and share the hour with the audience and just tell the truth. After that, I experimented with my stand-up style performance and slowly introduced the characters from my life. I easily spent three months trying to create some semblance of a Geordie accent for one teacher (I watched *Billy Elliot* and mimicked Julie Walters until I wasn't embarrassed by my efforts).

I was obsessed with the project. I collected hundreds of images and wrote all sorts of notes and thoughts. On my laptop I have a file full of what I like to call *The 100,000 Words of Chaos*. Even I cannot decipher it. It contains emotional entries, facts, copied web addresses and rants – all misspelt and lacking any form of sentence structure.

When I got round to making the whole show, the swiftly approaching deadline forced me to give up my fantasies of greatness. I was forced to relinquish the show in my head: the overly verbose one which made everyone think how clever and witty and charming I was. Instead, I realised that if I kept aiming for my idea of perfection, all I would have was that Word document and no show. So I had to let go. I put together the beginning, middle and end. The jokes were slotted in and I introduced animations and projections. The soundtrack was carefully selected to build nostalgia. I practised and then suddenly – it was opening night.

We sold out our first run. People turned up and there was laughter and tears (not just from me). It felt incredible to have something, to have made something from this experience. Each time I got up to start the show I would add jokes and pauses and experiment until I got the reaction I wanted. There were also bits that fell flat, places where I rushed and panicked. I still hadn't quite managed to hold my nerve. But most importantly of all, I knew it worked enough and I wanted to be able to show it to more people.

The Edinburgh Fringe Festival is the biggest international arts festival, which runs for the whole of August every year. It basically means that if you're in comedy or theatre you think it is the most important thing in the world. But if you're not, you've probably never heard of it. I certainly hadn't when I started at university. Pretty quickly, I gathered that all these people weren't just talking about the city of Edinburgh but something of *great cultural and social import.* Years before *K.O.* was even the seed of an idea, and part way through our degrees, Rachel ended up in Oxford's sketch comedy group and thus went up to Edinburgh for the whole month. I went and visited her in 2013. It was like I had been transported to some sort of adult endurance fairground. Everyone is vying for attention, audiences and ticket sales. I was completely overwhelmed and utterly taken in by the intensity. On the train back down to Leeds, I decided that I would take a show up there for the whole month, the following summer, by any means possible.

I managed it. Rachel persuaded the sketch troupe that I would be a great producer and so I found myself fully immersed this time for the duration of the Fringe. It simply solidified my addiction to the whole debacle. Each time I went I left with new missions. Next year I'll be performing, next year we'll break even, next year I'll have my own solo show, etc. etc.

Naturally, when the time came, not only was I determined to take *Everything is Going to be K.O.* to the Fringe, but I was determined to have it in a fancy prestigious venue. I had decided that this story of disability ought to be given that sort of treatment. It needed to be put on in a space that people respected because I believe the story should be respected.

The first year I applied, I was rejected by all the spaces I applied to. When I got the last rejection, I sobbed in the Chipotle by Tottenham Court Road on my lunch break before returning to my unpaid internship. After I had got over the initial shock, I had to look at why I hadn't been successful and started to plan again. This time I worked backwards, I needed to persuade them (the Establishment... the Gatekeepers... the actually lovely venue programmers) that I was a reliable set of hands. So we made a short film, we got some great press, I recorded a performance of the show. By the time the next year rolled round, I was applying with an armoury of tools. They offered me a slot. I sunk the little pot of money I had been saving from my wages into the deposit, and crossed my fingers.

By the time the August of the show came round, I was a wreck. My personal life had swiftly been pulled out from under my feet just weeks before. My long-term creative/business/romantic partner (yes, all the same person, I've learnt my lesson) and I had broken up, thus reminding us all not to mix professional endeavours with emotional turmoil. It was a fairly amicable breakup in the sense that I was utterly heartbroken but absolutely determined that nothing would get in the way of the show. I had worked too hard and too long on the project to let something as small as my world falling apart faze me.

I might have extolled the joys of the Fringe just paragraphs before this, but with all extreme highs comes the inevitable melodramatic lows. Due to the intensity, it can feel like you're trapped in a strange ego-destroying hellhole for a month. People talk about their success and you fret over losing all the money you had invested and you look at ticket sales and start to shake.

Even when you're doing well, you can fall into a trap of staying up late and surviving off the calorific intake of pints and packets of crisps. With hindsight, it is a miracle I made it through the month only slightly scathed and a few stone lighter.

It was a bad month by all standards. I had a screaming match with my ex on the Meadows where I graciously called the new woman in their life *a cunt bitch bastard.* I do regret that, I wish I had been more articulate. Then two weeks later, in the exact same spot, a man in a balaclava followed me, and my friends, Jasmine and Alex. I hadn't ever heard a punch land that clearly before. It was dull. The balaclava man had swung his fist into the back of Alex's head. Presumably, he had felt it was below even him to hit a woman. We ran home not even checking to see if we were followed. Alex didn't even once turn, he knew that there was no point, it would just escalate. I felt guilty that I was relieved; I had been certain it was going to end much worse than a mate getting thumped. Everyone else seemed to hold it together much better than I did.

Edinburgh wasn't all bad; my highlights included walking to M&S on my day off to buy new pants because I had run out and was certain doing a load of washing would finish me off. I had one really good crème brûlée. I lost my 'straight virginity' with a very beautiful twenty-one-year-old, finally proving that I'm the dictionary definition of a bisexual; I get laid twice a year. Like I say, it wasn't all bad.

I entirely put my survival down to the experience of performing the show every day. All I wanted to do was to remind the people in the same boat as me that they had a wealth of talents and skills in that brain of theirs. The very thing that might have meant that teachers and parents and co-workers had dismissed them is the thing that gives them their talents. I guess, I needed to hear it too.

The audiences for my show were wonderful. People were so generous. I got exactly what I asked for: stories. After the show, audience members would approach me and tell me about how they got to where they were in life. A successful retired businessman had been enterprising his own life since being kicked out of school as a teen. He had discovered his SpLDs aged sixty-five, when his young grandson got diagnosed. He and his wife had come to see me especially. After the show he exclaimed, *I'm clever and I've never thought of myself as clever before!* We had a photo taken together and I wish I had a copy of it. One woman had changed how she worked in an office. She had stood up to a bullying boss after he had picked on her. I was inspired by her tenacity. Another man told me about his time in the military and the problems they had with dyslexics and codes. There was even someone who had gone to Batley Grammar three decades before me in my audience. Strangers actually cried on my shoulder. I could never have anticipated the reaction I received. I was surprised to discover that my audience were mainly middle-aged men and they were wonderful, generous and weepy.

There have been many, many points in the process of making this book and the show in which I have staggered under the weight of my own ridiculous expectations. I wonder whether I have *anything worth saying or hearing.* Art, stories and even the humanities can seem so wishy-washy in the face of political upheaval, hatred towards the disabled and institutional failings. It can feel sometimes that I ought to be campaigning or doing something more concrete. But the problem is that I'm no good at the organising and the required institutional wrangling, and if I'm entirely honest I feel completely overwhelmed by the world of politics. Demonstrations are not the best place for me because of the inevitable sensory overload. Telling stories and making people laugh/cry are the things I'm good at. This is the method I have and it helps us feel less alone and it is itself a call to action. It might seem like a tiny thing, but in fact it is a matter of survival.

The voices of the people who message me to tell their stories or saying that they read articles I have written are the petrol in my tank. So I must thank every single person who has got in contact with me. Sometimes it's easier to do the work when you think about other people. Cutting it away from the personal and looking at it as a task for the collective stops you whacking out your own flame. But I have to stop and say, this is for me too. I earned it.

When I got back to London in September, I no longer had the show to pin my future on. It felt like a big breakdown or episode was circling, waiting for the chance to pluck me up and take me to what felt like inevitable insanity. Just as it always happens, when it feels like it can't get any worse, it does. More shit hit the fan and I stopped sleeping. I didn't know how I was going to pay the rent, where I was going to live or why I was really even bothering with this whole bloody business. Mum told me, *Just hold on; you don't know what's around the corner.*

She was right. Months later, I had signed a book deal and was bathed in the relief that I know nothing of the future. For the process of this book, my responsibility, luckily, has been looking at the past. I have been tasked with looking over my life so far and asking, how did I get here? Who am I? Who has taken this winding course, and what can it tell me about taking the next steps forward?

Words can feel so futile,
well at least to me. They are
devices I have to squash and stumble with to try to
form my story. I love the act of writing. Even though
it isn't necessarily easy, it is magical to push the mush
of my brain through the sieve of language and its
rules. The final product I hope is smooth and silky,
but in reality the product of all my efforts is lumpy
and chunky. I cannot easily make a perfect sentence,
I cannot squeeze my experience into the constraints
of the wiggly lines and symbols. Letters will never
be able to hold the cacophony that bubbles within
me. Maybe if I were able to sit and craft for another
six months and then another six years drafting and
scrapping I would have a little perfectly formed pebble
of a story for you. But I don't want to do that. It would
be somewhat dishonest and all too glib.

While writing the book, people have been asking
me what it is like to write with dyslexia (etc.). The
main piece of advice I have is *Do not read your work
back immediately.* Of course, maybe my experience
is not representative to all. But I have found that it is
a sure-fire way to stamp out the flame of creativity.
If I arduously pore over each word, going over each
sentence as I write, I become heavy with my own
inadequacy. It takes the fun out of spewing myself
onto keyboard or my journal or whatever receipt I
find in my pocket when I have a thought.

Since freeing myself of the constraints of trying to make good sentences straight away, I find that creativity now feels like a type of possession to me. I write and I try not to judge or think about it. It is a process of letting myself be. Craftsmanship is something I admire in other artists but I seem to struggle to master. Instead, making feels like something that is not my own. I do not have ownership of the drudgery of creation. It is something hardwired into me that it is my job to honour. Stories and characters and jokes pop up and ask to be written. It is not my job to decide if it is of value. It is my job to make sure that it exists. To get the words on the page rather than to sit in bed at night wondering what my book might look like. To put the hours into typing, into drawing and drafting. My role is that of a vessel.

I guess in many ways I subscribe to a classical idea of inspiration in the form of the Muses. But really all of this is a way of rationalising my own selfish desire to create something. It prevents me from looking at what I write and spitting on it. It stops me from saying that what I write is shit, that I'm shit, and I can't spell and have rudimentary understanding of grammar. Instead, I just think *Oh good, I needed to get that out of me and now it's on the page.* It's also a solid way of avoiding developing an ego because I am a high-risk candidate of being a self-aggrandising git. It is a pragmatic solution to a complex question of the cruel self-talk and self-sabotage which would rather that I sit down and shut up. But alas, silence isn't my style.

Obviously, memoir makes you ripe for contemplation. I guess the retiring, the pregnant and the dying are other groups of people who probably spent as much time in their own company as I have in the period of writing this, wrestling with the events that have befallen me. I'm already infinitely fascinated by myself, which is lucky because there isn't going to be an opportunity to drop me and start afresh with a new self (sorry, spoiler alert).

I went back to Batley for this book. Not to write the whole thing – I'm not a complete masochist – just for a day, here and there. I went back and spoke to my history teacher and to get my old reports. I was returning to a slightly changed place. Something dreadful had happened in the years since I left. Our MP, Jo Cox, had been murdered. When it happened I thought a lot about the segregation of the various parts of the community and the bubbling undertones of hatred. I always try to keep abreast of the local news. A child-grooming gang who were in operation in my school days were taken to court. These were the things that used to stick in my mind when I thought about Batley.

But going back I remembered other things – going to Muslim assembly to hear Muneeb reading from the Quran and nearly crying when I heard how his voice sung, or how kids used to try to throw water bottles at the low-flying seagulls above the school fields. Talking to Mr Hussain, I realised that I had not imagined the hostility I experienced from some pupils and teachers. I was vindicated. It also confirmed the strength of the support I got from him and Mrs Wilson was far far more powerful than any adversity.

I returned to my reports from school. They're better than I remembered. Lots of teachers seemed to like me. But there is an entire thread of English reports which bring up time and time again my ability to speak and communicate being vastly superior to my written ability. Now I read it and see them as almost dictionary definitions of my SpLD profiles. It was there, no one saw it.

I had been back to Oxford too, for a seemingly too-soon reunion. I rashly attended and on walking up Broad Street on the September morning I wished I had remained a recluse. It is funny how just returning to a place can suddenly cause you to regress. Just the sight of the faces of people I hadn't missed instantly pushed me back into my slightly rude and brusque eighteen-year-old self. It was all redeemed when I sat for lunch next to the tutor who had half a decade before, sent me for my diagnosis. We ate and debriefed. I thanked her because, really, that little thought of hers, which she could have easily forgotten or pushed aside, changed a lot for me.

I know now that quite a few adults and teachers in my life had briefly thought that maybe I had some sort of SpLD. But nothing had ever caused them the concern to say so. I know now that is why I slipped through the gaps. Partly, a lack of knowledge and understanding, and partly because I seemed to be doing fine. But Dr Kearns realised something quite special: that I was not fulfilling my potential.

As a result of that thought, my internal life radically changed. It triggered a long process of reflection. Each little story in this book is a scene I have played out and wondered how it fits into my life. Some have shaken my foundations and others seem obvious little skits.

The things I know to be true are that I have held my head high in the face of opposition and softened at the many kindnesses I have received. I have worked hard and I have at all times tried to know myself and love as much as possible.

For each revelation, I have stumbled and quivered and shouted *Who am I then?* Although this journey has not been easy or always fun, I am thankful to Dr Kearns for starting it and I am even more thankful that it set me on the path of this story. And at the very least it's all been good material.

It is a great honour to be neurodivergent. I am an old friend of chaos and failure. For that I am fortunate, because whoever you are, life is sending both of those to us all. Thinking differently has given me the tools to face chaos and failure. While I might not flourish in the tiny constraints of an office job or in exams or little forms full of boxes, I'm too busy for all that. I'm making my own weird winding path. My brain has allowed me to take each little step to the life I want now. My achievements have occurred not in spite of being neurodivergent but because I am.

Everything is always working out for me. Sometimes it settles my anxious heart to imagine that we are in a multiverse and this specific one I'm in is the path where everything works out the best it ever could, not just in the short term but the entire passage of my life. It also helps to remember that we're on a winding journey. There's no point aiming for the big break or winning in the end because, really, with life there's only one climax for us all – dying. That isn't to say that it doesn't hurt when things go badly and you fail. Pain is pain. No amount of thinking and logistical gymnastics can take you out of that. But I try to make my past survival a beacon of hope for myself. The shit stuff has put me on paths I could never have imagined. The flame in my belly has never gone out.

So when I reflect on the astounding talents of people like me and not like me, whose brains work a little differently, I am set aflame. Our society and the way that we measure success, value and merits is so constrictively small. In schools, workplaces and our own homes, when we tell people that they are lazy or stupid or a disappointment we fail to see the great potential in them.

When we put out our own fires or stamp out those of other people, we do a disservice to everyone. The whole world misses out when kids (and adults) don't get to fulfil their potential, or our own narrow views of things limit the numinous possibilities available.

Neurodivergence is an incredible gift from which we can all benefit. The insights, patterns and world views offer up originality and innovative thinking – something we desperately need in this swiftly changing world.

It is not enough that I succeeded, by getting to Oxford or publishing this book. It is not enough if you, reading this book, manage to find your own path. Because, if things were slightly different, we could have failed and there are many other people who have fallen through the gaps. It helps that I'm white and young and able-bodied, it would have been an even greater task if any of those things had been different. We need to look outwards and ask why there are so few of us succeeding in spite of the system and demand that the established institutions make the necessary changes.

The people who are in charge of how the world is run have no impetus to change it because it has suited them just fine, it got them to those positions of power, even though it's now fashionable for people in power to feign wokeness. It is those people who decide how our education system is set up and they cannot see the power of harnessing neurodivergence because their world view is so small. They see test results, Ofsted reports, employment figures, profits, efficiency numbers, data. They are blind to the kid who can feel colours and writes the poetry that makes you feel less alone. They ignore the girl whose understanding of space and patterns is so extraordinary that she can predict the future or at least the next steps in mechanical engineering. They fail to support the adult learner with life experience and a desire to immerse themselves in education in order to improve themselves for no other reason than that it is a worthy ambition to want more and to want differently.

The consequence of such amputation of our collective potential is enormous. With derision, quiet sarcasm and violent criticism comes the destruction of our future. Books go unwritten, songs stay stuck in throats and ideas become squashed into self-hatred. Loud, bristling personalities are asked to be less, to calm down, to fit into the tiny limits of accepted beauty. Then quiet, burgeoning individuals are told to push forward, stamp, trample their way to be heard rather than asking the world to listen and accept the hushed breath of their existence.

The most deeply cruel violence of all is that we are taught to pass it on. We are trained to enact that same assault upon ourselves to repeat back what we were told before. Echoing the words of the past, we limit and lessen who we are and our complexity. We can hold the multitudes: difficulties and strengths, joys and sorrows, pasts and futures. The rebellion comes in refusing to participate in the severing of yourself, in seeing just one tiny fragment and then investing in your own and others' excellence.

All I can say right now, is that I see you and I see the fire in your belly. I ask you to see that potential in yourselves and the people around you. Like historical beacon chains, when we see someone else's fire, we should take comfort and joy in the symbolic communication. You're here and I'm here. The success of those around me is not something to make me feel sad but rather something to ignite passion. Seeing the incredible potency of the people around you is a sure-fire way of transforming the world for the good.

Because it is not enough to say that everything is going to be OK. OK is too small and too passive for us. We are more than that and we want a better, bigger future for ourselves. So we must strive for something else. Demand more.

Everything is going to be enlightening, incredible, heartbreaking, ace, annihilating, awesome, unbearable, wicked, painful, joyful, unimaginable, magic.

Everything is going to be knock-out.

EPILOGUE

EPILOGUE

As a child, I had largely been unimpressed by pets. I had a younger brother who fulfilled my desire for a cute sidekick. Plus, the goldfish we did have never did much more than swim in their own shit and, at their most exciting, die. Once levelling up to teenager, I became determined that what I needed was a cat. I had watched enough anime and read more than enough manga to realise that I needed an adorable little creature to offset my personal failings. Cas was too old and definitely no longer interested in tagging along snapping at my heels. Initially, I liked the idea of a pet squirrel but I was assured they couldn't be tamed. It was the dawn of the Internet era, I can has cheeseburger, cat videos and memes. The RSPCA couldn't have come up with a more effective PR campaign if it had tried. A cat it had to be.

My parents have always had a fairly blanket rule on pets – *if it arrives on the doorstep starving, you can keep it.*

It is a cruel answer. Not a direct *no, give up, it isn't happening.* Instead, it is a hope-giving answer. There is the tiniest possibility of it happening. More than just that, as the myth goes, a pregnant dog had arrived on my mother's doorstep when she had been a kid. They had named her Beauty. She woofed at the door to go out and would take herself on walks. There is just no beating that – the pet that looks after themselves.

My friend at the time joked about buying a kitten and dropping it off on the doorstep. But I was staunchly against it; that would be cheating and, more importantly, we lived on a main road and I couldn't have a squished kitten on my conscience. Being a teenager was tricky enough without being haunted by the ghost of a cat waffled by the tread of a boy racer's Fiat Punto.

I tried my fail-safe method of fantasy. In the car to school, I would recount stories of the adventures of my imaginary pet cat. His name was Mooney and he was all black because, remember, I was an emo. He would sneak about and burgle the houses of rich old ladies. I would hoard the jewels he dropped into my palms from his soft mouth. With our winnings, we would buy a motorbike and Mooney would naturally ride in the sidecar. My parents love that imagination shit.

They would lap this up and I'd have a real Mooney by the end of the year.

But that Christmas, my parents kept giggling – in that sort of gross way that parents do to remind you that they still love each other and have sex. I was naturally repulsed but glad that they were having fun. Soon I realised that the laughter was coming from some sort of inside joke. On Christmas morning I opened my usual haul of books and clothes (all I ever want) and I came to the last present. It was box-shaped. It was woefully too small to be a kitten, even one with dwarfism like Grumpy Cat. I opened it up to reveal a mug.

Now, I love a good mug, in fact some of my most prized possessions are mugs (shout out to Nick for my new favourite K-pop merch). I drink a lot of tea and I collect dirty cups in my room like a twelve-year-old boy collects Pokémon cards. *Gotta catch 'em all!* So I had nothing against the principle of the present. My problem was the print on the mug. It read: *Only my cat understands me.*

Boy, did my parents laugh and laugh. They thought they were so funny, so witty, so astute. You see, dear readers, I had no cat. So NO ONE UNDERSTOOD ME! It was a phrase I had frequently shouted down the stairs at them on a weeknight. It mocked both my petlessness and my completely unoriginal teenage shit fits. It was the perfect gift.

New year came and went. It was one of those old winters we used to have before the planet began melting – it snowed. Normally, we parked our car behind our house on the little lane before Dog-Shit Park (aka Needle-Trash Walk) which overlooked our road. But snow meant ice and the road was unsafe to drive down. So my parents parked on the main road in front. One snowy day, they came back from doing The Big Shop all excited, more excited than one might expect even after a trip down the Tesco Extra.

There's a white cat at the front door!

Cas and I ran and looked out the window. There was. It was scrappy and sort of ugly and angrily meowing. If it was speaking I think it would have been saying *FEED ME, YOU IGNORANT BASTARDS.* This was everything I had ever dreamt of but I wasn't excited or happy, I was just completely terrified.

We fed the cat a tin of crab meat that was in the cupboard and my dad wondered why on earth we even had it. The cat yammed it down so quickly we were left in no doubt that it was starving. It then vommed up the food as quick as it had wolfed it down. We made a little bed for it in the porch. *It's pregnant and it was dumped by its owner,* Wizzy theorised, *but it's winter so we shouldn't have to worry about fleas.* Cas and I improvised names, growing more and more adventurous with the cat until it went to bite us. Whatever

EMPTY BELLY

its history, it was very defensive.  We were warned: *It's a wild animal. It can leave whenever it wants. It might only want to stay while it snows.*

Eventually the weather thawed and the cat managed to keep down its food. Dad wrapped it in a towel and took it to the vet. The cat returned, unpregnant and thoroughly de-flead. We named him Zeus because of the black marks on the top of his head in the shape of a three-pronged socket, and the link between electricity and the king of the gods' lightning bolt was too satisfying to let slide.

He never did leave us. Zeus was his own creature, certainly, but as the years passed he softened. Eventually, he would let himself be stroked, then picked up and finally he fell into a routine of affection. I wouldn't say he was a pet because, like every member of my family, he was thoroughly untamed.

I used to imagine the journey he'd been on before he arrived with us, travelling around the world and participating in famous events. He'd been an Egyptian prince, of course, but did you know he was the mascot at the first silent film studios? He had curled up with children in workhouses and tripped up servants in the Palace of Versailles. Zeus had inspired the invention of the croissant and bitten the hands of more than one emperor.

He is my mascot, which is why he peppers my illustrations. The white shiny bitey knight. He represents that magic of the unknown and the unexpected.

He died a few years ago from a heart problem. He miraculously survived three cardiac events in total, each time defying everyone's expectations. When he did die, he fell asleep on my parents' bed and never woke up (which I guess is the definition of death). But it doesn't really feel like he has gone anywhere.

It is not lost on me that the publisher of this book is called Head of Zeus. My agent excitedly told me, thinking the classics connection big enough. But I knew that something wonderful was around the corner with that news. I imagined Zeus setting off to work at his own independent publishers in a bowler hat and insisting that they *Make this book happen!* In my funny brain, this is another connection and another plot point in Zeus' story and my own. A big overarching spider web of the outside world and my internal narrative woven together to make life seem that bit more magical. It's another story constructed out of seeing patterns and ties in the world around me, a true product of neurodivergence.

ACKNOWLEDGEMENTS

This book has been a shared labour.

Firstly, without my agent, Marianne Gunn O'Connor and her unwavering belief in both this project and in me, I would have long since given up on this book. She is magic.

I must thank my editors, Ellen Parnavelas, Florence Hare and Madeleine O'Shea, for their wonderful support. Special thanks go to Ben Prior for a beautiful cover and layout. I appreciate the whole team at Head of Zeus for all their work.

Then of course, I'm grateful to all those who made the earlier versions of KO possible. The show and short film were the precursor and without their help there would be no book in your hands now: Jessy Parker Humphreys, the staff at both the Pleasance and Theatre Royal Stratford East, The Old Vic New Voices Scheme, Daisy Hale, Arlen Figgis, Simji Park, Canvas and Arts Council England.

I am incredibly grateful to my chosen kin for the pints, dinners, dancing, late night phone calls and generally for making sure I'm still here and kicking: Rachel (& Claire, Colin and Michael), Jasmine, Emilia, Connie, Rivka, Guan, Nick & Paddy, Anna, Laura and Lydia (& all the Brewdog gang). Then of course, I am forever indebted to Jamie Carragher whose help was instrumental in improving this book and who always makes writing a less lonely pursuit.

Shout-out to the great teachers: Janice Wilson, Tariq Hussain, Sharon Kennard, Emily Kearns, Rebecca Armstrong, Katherine Clarke, Fiona Macintosh, Brian Astbury & The Forge Initiative, Marcus J Richardson and Ariane Mnouchkine & the Théâtre du Soleil. And big love to all my pupils and their families who have given me a new perspective on education: Charlie (and Louise), Morgan & Delphi (and Claire), Kate, Hannah, Logan and Gloria.

My deepest gratitude to Alastair for the roof over my head which has made writing this book possible.

Cheers to my big fucked up extended family.

Finally, there would be not a single word without Adam, Wilma and Casius Stone; Everything I do is in honour of you.

Kaiya Stone is a writer, performer, and director who likes to tell stories any way she can. She snuck her way out of Yorkshire into the hallowed halls of Oxford University only to discover that she had many undiagnosed learning difficulties. She turned this experience into a one-woman show which debuted at the Theatre Royal Stratford East and then ran at Edinburgh Festival 2018. *Everything Is Going To Be K.O.* is her first book.

🐦 @Kaiya_stone